The Maypole Corollary

A Memoir of Love
By Rene Sutherland

I believe everyone has a unique and important story to tell. This is mine and I dedicate it to my Mama and Papa, who made me and this story possible.

The

Maypole

Corollary

Dear 40 year old parent and miracle child,

My parents were in their middle 40's at the time of my birth. It is what makes me unique. Today, that is not a very unique experience, but in the 1960's it was rare. My parents were the age of ALL my friends' grandparents. I have spent my entire life thinking about what it means to have older parents. I have appreciated the good times and I have cried through the difficult times. I write this book for the parent who had the courage to have a child later in life and for the miracle child in search of understanding. I encourage compassion, tolerance and hope to inspire thought about how we view life stages.

Sincerely,

Love

Contents

Part I

Part II

Part 1

Chapter 1

Wisdom; the Fifth Life Stage

"Good Morning, Papa. I love you."

"Rene, he's not breathing very well. It sounds so laborious. He did alright last night, but just about a half hour ago his breathing changed. What do you think we should do?"

"Oh, ok, Mama; I'll swab his mouth out.
Oh gosh, I'm getting a lot of mucus out. It's really thick. I think I should call the hospice nurse."

"Hi, Gail; this is Rene Sutherland. My Dad's breathing seems to be really laborious; it's almost a gurgle. He has a lot of mucus in his throat. I have been swabbing his throat, but it doesn't seem to be doing much good. If we elevate his bed more upright would that help perhaps?"

20

"Rene, he's on the runway; he's going to be dying soon. That is what we call the death rattle. If you have family you need to call, now is the time."

"Oh. Ok. Is there anything we should do different from what we are doing?"

"No. You're doing a good job keeping him comfortable. He knows that you are there and that you love him. That's really all that you can do."

"Ok, thank you. Good bye."

The sun is streaming through the open window onto my Papa's bare chest and arms. His body is sparkling in the sun from the perspiration droplets forming all over him. It is a clear blue day and the Pacific Ocean is shining brilliantly. The breeze feels good but I don't think he can feel it anymore. I don't think he is enjoying the sun on his body, like he used to on those hot summer days at the lake. I lower the shades. He is dying and the glorious beauty of this world has already faded away from behind his eyes. His world is his own now. He is leaving us.

"Mama, I'm going to call Diane. I think she should start driving up here."

"What do you mean? What did the hospice nurse say? Why does Diane need to come up?"

"Mama, I think Papa's dying right now."

"Oh God, no."

"I'm sorry Mama. I think that gurgle we hear means he is leaving us."

"Oh no, Rene, no."

"Connie, can you come down here? We need to be next to Papa now."

"Papa, we love you. We're here with you."

"Carl, honey, I'm here, my love."

There is an intensity that is building; each breath is a

gasp grasped out of the air as though stolen without permission. Each breath is quicker and deeper. Each breath he takes takes him away from us and brings him closer to God.

"Papa, I love you"

"Oh, Carl, my one and only love; I love you Carl."

"It's ok Papa. It's ok."

"I love you, Papa."

"We love you, Papa."

"It's ok Papa. It's ok. It's ok Papa. It's ok. We know you need to go now, Papa. We'll be alright. We love you so much."

It's that final moment. We are there holding him, placing our hands on his chest as it heaves up and down, holding his arms, stroking his face and head. His eyes are open but he cannot see us. He is looking upward but it is not our space that he sees.

He is seeing into Heaven.

He is leaving us.

His gasps become weaker.

He is slowing down.

My Mama looks at us in disbelief.

Her heart is breaking.

His pupils open up as though they are absorbing the universe.

My Mama is collapsing against his bare chest.

She is dying along with him.

And then he's gone.

His chest does not move.

My Papa is gone.

His life is no more.

My Papa is gone.

Chapter 2

First Life Stage: Natural Simplicity

My heart beats with appreciation and it is my strength when all else fails

I had a wonderful childhood. I knew it at the time and I appreciated it every second of every day. The greatest gift I received from having older parents is my ability to appreciate my life and the people I have in my life. My heart beats with appreciation and it is my strength when all else fails.

I was a young girl extremely well loved but scared I might lose my parents. I learned to be brave young and to rely on knowing my parents loved me very much and with love I would make it through anything. I grew up thanking my parents for being so wonderful. I told my Mommy every day, if not five times a day, how much I loved her. I got home from my school day and sat on my Mommy's lap and said to her,

"I love YOU more than you love me!!"

"Oh no, no, no; I love YOU more than you love me!" She'd reply.

This little play with words got our bellies rolling with laughter; a little battle of love.

I was a very sweet child. I attribute my sweetness to my parent's show of love for me. They were older and felt very lucky to have me in their lives.

"Little one, come here."

Daddy patted his leg. I ran over and climbed up high and gave him a big hug.

"You give your Mommy and me so much happiness. Do you know how much we love you?"

"Yes!" I would say with a big smile.

"Good. It's very special and rare that Mommy and Daddy have you because we're older. I want you to always remember how much Mommy and Daddy love you, OK?"

"Ok Daddy. I love you!"

In the 1960's it was frowned upon for older parents to have children. My Mama's friends felt so sorry for her when they saw her pregnant at 44 years old,

"One Sunday I walked into church and the ladies were looking over at me. I thought they were admiring my hat I had made, but they were staring at my belly! The ladies couldn't believe I was pregnant.

'Aren't you scared?'

'Aren't you worried about the baby?'

I told them, 'God has a plan for us and I'm sure everything will be fine'."

Yes, of course my parents were concerned. It was common knowledge of the day that older parents were at a high risk of giving birth to a child with Down Syndrome; 1 in every 19. But my parents were not worried. They prayed I would be healthy, my Mama felt good and they knew whatever baby God gave them, they would love the baby no matter.

Later my Papa would joke with me and say,

"You don't know this little one, but you're actually a mongoloid child. You have old genes. That's why your eyes look like they do. Haven't you ever noticed?"

This little joke sounds terrible now; first, for calling a Down Syndrome child a mongoloid and, secondly, for joking about such a serious matter. But when a concern is stressful, making a joke of it relieves that stress.

Despite the risks, my parents were very excited to be having another child.

"Your Daddy's chest popped out two feet with pride. He thought it was the best thing on earth Mommy could be pregnant again!"

It was always apparent my parents felt extremely blessed I was healthy. And those feelings were transferred to me. The chances of me being born at all were quite slim and you could say I was something of a miracle. I believe most 40 year old parents believe their pregnancy is a miracle, a true blessing. I felt I had been given a chance at life and it was very important for me to appreciate that chance, that gift.

Appreciation is the strongest feeling in my heart. I appreciate the love I receive from my family. I appreciate the opportunity to love people back and to do things for them. I appreciate being needed by my family and being able to take care of them. I appreciate the beauty of this world and the people who live on this planet. I appreciate life because I was given life. This gift of appreciation in my heart is my parent's doing. Thank you, Mama and Papa; I appreciate you!

I appreciate everything you gave up in your older age in order to raise me. While your friends were traveling Mama, you were playing room mother in my classroom and putting on the Thanksgiving party for 30 fifth graders. While your friends were retiring Papa, you were working long hours at your office so you could spend time with us at the lake in the summer. I know you felt lucky to have me, but it must have been hard. It must have been hard, Papa, to look into your future, as you did so often, and think about how you were going to take care of me well into your 60's. People didn't live as long in your parents' generation and you really didn't feel confident you would make it past your 50's. You had fought in WWII and the Korean War and you were exposed to chemicals and toxins. I kept you young and on your toes because at the age of 45 you had to figure out how to put a child through college in your 60's. Instead of retiring you figured out how to make a new career in the stock market to have enough money for you, Mama and me. You provided for your family so well and you will always be my inspiration Papa. I miss you and love you so much. Thank you for everything you did for me.

It must have been tiring for you too, Mama, to wake up at all hours of the night with a newborn baby. I am 42 years old and I feel my age. I can't imagine what being pregnant feels like at 44. You always said I kept you young. Well, Mama, you are 87 years old and still playing tennis, so I guess you were right. All the running around after me and trying to keep up with a child made you strong and made you feel young. I used to think I wanted to have children when I was 45 years old because I saw how young you acted. Your friends seemed to be slowing down, but not you or Papa. You have always been active and I admire how you have a pep-in-your-step. I love you, Mama, so very much! Thank you for everything you did for me.

Good night, Rene. Sweet dreams

I vividly remember bedtime. I had my own room and it was next to my brother's room. He was 8 years older than me and got to stay up later. If I put my little ear next to the wall and listened really hard, I heard him talking on the phone. I strained to understand his words, but unfortunately the words were just muffled sounds. What I didn't have to work hard on hearing was his music,

"…the Midwest farmer's daughters, they make you feel alright and the Northern girls with the way they kiss they keep their boyfriends warm at night. I wish they all could be California…"

He loved the Beach Boys music and would listen to it on his reel to reel music machine every night.

My room was east facing and was very dark at night. I had my twin bed, my night stand with a lamp and my AM/FM clock radio set to Mighty 690 and, later in my preteens, to KROQ. While the stations changed as I grew older, my bedtime thoughts and prayers did not change. My prayer each night was this:

31

"If I die before I wake, I pray the Lord my soul to take. But please God, please, please don't take my Mommy or Daddy. Please!"

Mommy came in to kiss me goodnight each night and tuck me in to bed. I loved her so much it hurt. She came into the room, walked across the floor to the right side of my bed and looked down upon me as she said,

"Good night Rene. Sweet dreams."

"Hug….hug….please!"

"Oh, Mommy's too old to bend down so far."

"Please! Please!"

"Ok, but be gentle."

Mommy bent down and I wrapped my arms around her neck and pulled her down to me. I wanted her to lay with me and not go away. When I finally did let her go, she placed her right hand on the bed and pushed herself upright, smiled a loving, sweet Mommy smile and said,

"I love you! Now, good night."

"Good night, Mommy. I love you sooooooo much!!"

"Sweet dreams. Do you want the door open or closed?"

I saw her silhouette standing in the doorway; the hall light illuminating the background.

"Open, please."

And with that she left. I was left staring at the thin line of light coming through my partially opened door. Listening to her soft footsteps as she walked away, I felt a sense of loneliness creeping into my being. I heard sounds from my Papa's television in the living room. I felt the warm forced air coming through the ceiling vent and I saw the darkness; darkness so deep and heavy I could feel the pressure of it on my face. If I closed my eyes, I sensed the space coming in on me. I told myself its ok and everything would be ok. I calmed myself and tried to relax. Prayer gave me a sense of power over the future. If I prayed hard enough God would listen and everything would be ok.

"....Please, Lord, don't take my Mommy or Daddy...I'll be good, I promise...please, please, please."

Happy Birthday, Love

My childhood was different than my friends' childhoods. When children and parents met me they always thought I was with my grandparents. I thought it was very funny.

On my first day of Kindergarten I walked up the long outside stairs to the front door of my Kindergarten room where my Mommy and I were greeted by my new teacher, Mrs. Prester. She had a really big, bouffant hairdo, left over from the 1960's. She was pretty and nice. I was really nervous about my first day of school and was holding my Mommy's hand. I wasn't sure if I would let go of her hand or not, when Mrs. Prester walked over and said,

"Oh how lovely. What is your name?"

"Rene."

"And is this your Grandmother?"

"Noooo, this is my Mommy!"

"Oh! Pardon me. I'm sorry."

My Mommy accepted the apology; she was used to it, and started talking about the day's events.

Funny grown-ups! They were so silly to think my Mommy was my Grandma. Hadn't they ever seen my Grandma? She had grey hair and was old and wrinkly! Of course my Mommy wasn't my Grandma! My Mommy had blonde hair, played tennis and was really sweet.

My eyes quickly moved passed the grown-ups and out toward the playground. I saw the other children playing and so I darted past the teacher to the swings outside under the big Oak tree.

I was very lucky to have my parents because life was pretty good for them by the time I came around and I benefitted from their financial security and emotional stability. However, I did notice that my parents were not as young and active as other children's parents. My parents owned a mobile home at Lake Havasu at the end of the island by the airport. We went there for several months every summer and on Holidays too. I have a clear memory of watching a family play in the pool one day. The father and mother were young, tall and beautiful. They had two children, one being a girl named Summer. They were from Rolling Hills, wherever that was. I watched, mesmerized, as the father picked up the little girl, high above his head and gently tossed her into the pool. I watched and watched. Finally I couldn't take it anymore and asked,

"Excuse me; will you do that to me?"

"Of course I will!"

I spent the rest of the day playing with Summer from Rolling Hills. I was really fascinated with this family. My Daddy was still strong when I was little. We had a pool in our own backyard and he had me stand on his shoulders while he held my hands, then he would throw me up into the air using his leg strength. I loved playing with him in the pool. He threw me and my friends and we had a lot of fun. But this Daddy of Summer's held us straight up in the air with his arms! He probably was 30 years old and in his prime. This was an age that I could not imagine my parents to ever have been. My parents were old for my entire life. I cannot picture them young. I have heard many stories from them and my siblings, but they are other people's memories, not mine. This sometimes bothered my Papa. He would say to me,

"I wish you could have seen your Papa when he was young! Why, I used to have your one sister on one leg and your other sister on the other leg and laying on the bed in the morning, I used to swing them around like a propeller on an airplane!"

I really noticed the age difference between my parents and my best friend Chrissy's parents because I played with her every day. Her parents were closer in age to my sister than to my Mommy and Daddy. It put a lot of questions in my little brain. When I was 4 years old I asked my Daddy if he would always be my

Daddy. We were on our way to the lake. I can picture leaning over the driver's seat and asking him quietly in his right ear,

"Daddy, I want you to be with me forever. Will you always be my Daddy?"

He said to me,

"Come here, little one. I have a secret for you."

With that I climbed up and over the middle seat and snuggled up against him.

"I will always be here for you and you never need to worry because I have a special name for you, 'Love.' And on your 50th birthday I will be right next to you, to watch you blow out your candles and I will say, 'Happy Birthday, Love'."

So, I didn't need to worry anymore because that is how it would be. I love him so much for telling me that secret and calling me "Love" for the rest of his life.

Olive party

I grew up in a neighborhood full of kids. Every house had four or more kids, except for the Alperts next door, they only had three kids and I felt sorry for them. As early as I can recall, I remember trying to hang out with the older kids and being denied.

We lived by the college and the college's football, track, baseball and soccer field were found in the valley below our street. I grew up in an interesting neighborhood. Although we were in Los Angeles County and our town was close to some pretty rough towns, our street itself was a dead end street nestled up in the hills. I grew up hiking and playing in what I thought was the wilderness. I listened to coyotes at night and unfortunately for my kitties, the coyotes often came into our backyard. We found rattlesnakes, king snakes, raccoons and possums in our pool all the time. We didn't have bears but I know that we had mountain lions; luckily for me I never came across any.

My street consisted of about 21 houses that I considered part of the neighborhood. Beyond that we had a network of about 7 streets that looped through the steep hills and where we considered kids our playmates. We kids called ourselves, for fun, the "Hadley Hills Locals," when we were in high school. Although when we were little runts, we just knew we lived up the long, super steep hill that we had to drag ourselves up after a fun day walking around down town.

Because my siblings were older, I had a feeling I was more like an only child on my own than a child that was a part of a family with brothers and sisters. My friends were either fighting or laughing with their siblings and I never really had that experience. I did fight with my older brother once in a while but in all honesty he always won. I was no match for a boy 8 years older than me. He was more of my protector when I was a little girl than anything. I guess you could say my siblings were like extra parents.

One day in particular sticks in my mind. The entire neighborhood seemed to be out playing and as usual I tried to join the fun. I was only five years old and I was just a little girl to them. I was tall for my age and skinny. I had blond, curly, sometimes frizzy, hair. My hair was so light blond that when the sun was shining on me, my hair became see-through and it gave me a certain weird head glow. It was summer so I was in my favorite summer dress. It was a dress only a little girl can wear; where the bottom of the dress falls just below your bottom and when you roll around on the grass your little white undies with a daisy flower pattern shows to the world. The kids were going to walk down to the college field and I wanted to go with them. They didn't want me to follow and let me know it in no uncertain terms. Perhaps they were going to hide and smoke cigarettes but I was too young to understand that kind of stuff. All I knew was I was alone and I wanted to play with someone. So on that summer day, in my little summer dress, I followed.

The kids often teased me and taunted me and this day was no different. I had learned to deal with my brother teasing me and felt I could stick up for myself. As we walked down the street toward the dirt path that led through the ravine to the field, they kept chanting to me,

"Baby talk, baby talk, it's a wonder you can walk."

They often sang this until I was in tears running home, but on this day I was determined to not go home and to follow them the rest of the day. I wanted to have fun too! As we walked down the dirt road they began, one by one, turning around and singing,

"Baby talk, baby talk, it's a wonder you can walk. Go home little baby before you get in trouble!"

They tried to make me cry by singing their song. They tried to scare me and say I would get in trouble for going so far from home. They tried to be mean and make me leave, but I wouldn't stop walking and following behind them. Finally, they turned around and made me go home. They all walked me to my house and then started yelling at me,

"Go inside and don't follow us!"

"We don't want you with us!"

My brother came outside to find them yelling at me and me crying. He picked up olives that had fallen from our tree, onto the driveway, and chucked them at the kids. He threw so many olives for such a long time, the kids tried to hit him back but he was just that much older than them that their efforts were fruitless. He beaned each and every one of them! I looked at my big brother that day and felt so lucky to have him. I may have been the baby of the family and I may not have had a sibling near my age to hang out with, but on that day I did have someone who cared about me enough to not care that the neighborhood kids would hate him from that day forward. And that felt awesome.

I never tried to follow the kids again. Their meanness had finally made an impact on me; I never wanted kids to be able to treat me like that again. I didn't know if I was dumb for talking differently and being different or if I was really smart. Either way, my world seemed unlike theirs. Somehow I just didn't fit in; I was unaware of a rule or a protocol when it came to playing with a group of kids. Perhaps they were afraid of me telling on them because I was little, but no matter the reason, I was somewhat of a loner when I was young. That's probably why I chose two friends, Chrissy and her brother, Tim, and stuck with them. I was a loyal friend. I had known Chrissy and Tim my whole life. Chrissy was my age and Tim was one year older. We were playpen buddies. The three of us played every day; we had clubs and forts, made up our own songs and games. Since other kids had their siblings to stick up for them, I fastened myself onto Chrissy and Tim and became their sibling.

One day Chrissy was over playing with me on my swing set. She noticed the black "Happy Birthday" balloons and the signs that said, "Over the Hill!" We were celebrating my Daddy's birthday and she asked,

"How old is your Daddy?"

"Oh, he's 50 today."

"Nu-uh! He can't be 50."

"Why can't he be 50?"

"You mean he's 30. He has to be 30 because my parents are 30."

"Ohhh…maybe…but my sisters are 20. I don't think he's 30. But maybe he's 40."

Looking back, it's funny to remember how confusing it was at times. I had to figure out my parents were older.

Shortly after the olive incident the Foresters moved away. The older boy in that family was the lead kid, a bit of a bully. A quieter family, the Abrahamians, with one boy, one girl named Carol, and a Siberian husky, moved into the Forester's old house. Carol's house had a pool, as did mine, but Carol's mom bought really good snack food and candy and soda and mine did not. My mom was old school and sent children home to eat. It was a left over reaction to the Great Depression, when families had so little that children were taught to not eat other peoples' food. Chrissy started spending more time over at Carol's. It wasn't Chrissy's fault; her tummy liked being at Carol's house more than at my house. I was sad to see my friend leave me for another friend. I don't know why kids have a hard time playing together, but it seems that whenever you get three kids together, one gets left out.

One day in particular was really bad. Chrissy was over and we were in my pool swimming. We started talking about how Carol always had a lot of licorice at her house and how her mom made sandwiches and let the kids eat from the big bag of chips. Chrissy was sitting next to me on the stoop in the deep end of the pool and suddenly got up,

"I'm tired of swimming and I'm hungry. I'm gonna go to Carol's house."

"But you said you were gonna spend the night."

Chrissy shrugged and said nothing.

"Please don't go."

"I'm going. You can't stop me!"

With that, I remember running over to Daddy, crying. Daddy told Chrissy that it wasn't nice to leave one friend and say you're going to another friend's house. Chrissy got scared and started crying and I started crying more; the whole thing was emotional. Chrissy did go home after that and I was sad. I don't think I ever, ever told on anyone again. It didn't pay off and I felt lousy for getting my Daddy involved. I remember feeling in a panic when I ran to my Daddy. I wanted him to make her stay, but he couldn't. He knew that, of course, but I had to learn. From then on I have always known you can't change someone's mind; they will do what they want to do. Later in life, I would watch as people thought they were changing others, only to watch the other person do it behind that person's back. People will do what they want to do; one way or another. So I learned early on to let go and not try to control someone. We were only seven when Chrissy and I fought that day and Chrissy's parents were fighting a lot during those years, so she was going through some very rough times; isn't that usually the case? Often times we take something personally, only to find out that the other person has something on their mind and they don't mean to hurt us. Now when someone is being mean to me, I slow down and wonder what perhaps could be going wrong in their life. Perhaps, instead of getting mad, I should offer a helping hand and ask,

"Is there anything I can help you with today?"

Or straight out say,

"You're sounding anxious to me. Is there something that has happened that we can talk about?"

You would be amazed how many times a person will open up and share a stressful worry. Then you can work through it together.

Chrissy and I recovered quickly from our fight and, instead of fighting, we spent most of our time running around the hills, jumping off of walls with our umbrellas in the rain and swimming in the creek while we pretended to be Amazons. My fondest early childhood memories include Chrissy and Tim; I am so thankful for their friendships. When we were in fifth grade, her parents divorced and she moved away. She moved to a house closer to our school so I still got to see her, but we were never as close as we were when we were little. After high school, we lost track of each other, almost… we hooked back up for each of our weddings and we both named our baby girls' middle names after each other, without the other knowing until years later. When you are such good friends, you are friends for life, whether you see each other or not.

After Chrissy moved away, her house stayed vacant for a little while. Then at the end of sixth grade I noticed a family moving into Chrissy's house. I was so excited. I grabbed my new 45 record, "Whip It" by Devo, and ran down to ask the new girl, Mary, if she wanted to walk downtown and return my 45 with me because it was scratched. She did and we became great friends.

Another neighborhood friend was Sharise who lived next door to Mary, as she had for many years lived next door to Chrissy. Sharise had a pool with a really cool slide but a newer diving board that wasn't bouncy. When we were little and Chrissy lived next door, we would figure out whose pool we were going to swim in by first figuring out what we wanted to play because my pool had a really long, really bouncy diving board. By the time Mary moved in next door, things were changing. Something was happening in our neighborhood. Families were changing in size. Two kids seemed to be the new norm. As we entered junior high school we were changing; we didn't swim in our pools anymore. We were too busy listening to music, watching MTV and talking about boys.

Mary and I went to the same junior high across town. I took the bus there until I was kicked off of the bus and my Mom had to drive me; she wasn't very happy about that one. Junior high was junior high. My school was huge and I only knew a fraction of the kids. It was a tough school with gangs and fights. I remember "Spider" beating a kid up right in front of my locker. I saw a knife in his hand but thankfully he didn't use it. I was friends with a lot of girls who were way tougher than me. They were hard core Cholas and they lived in neighborhoods where bars on the windows and doors were required. They were nice and I liked talking to them in class. But I learned I was not as tough as I thought I was. One girl in particular would call me every night and say she was going to beat me up the next day at school. I think she was lonely and just liked talking to me on the phone; she would threaten me just enough to make me keep trying to talk her out of beating me up. I was scared and she knew it. It took me all year to finally gather up enough courage to stand up to her. My brother was in college and taking a self-defense class. One night, he worked with me for an hour on how to kick someone right in the knee to break their leg; or so I thought he had taught me a skill. The next day, when she walked up to me and said she was going to beat me up, I said,

"Fine, let's go."

Confident I was able to defend myself, I faced her and called her bluff. Luckily, she wasn't expecting that and just turned around and walked away. She never did beat me up. It was the end of the school year and I didn't see her that summer or ever again. Violence, promiscuity and my friends looking forward to partying were the reasons I chose to go to a different high school.

The high school I went to was a private Catholic school with uniforms and a gate around the school. It was a strict school my sisters had attended twenty years earlier. By 1983 a lot had changed, the nuns were no longer allowed to hit you with their ruler for wearing your skirt too short, girls were allowed to walk and talk with boys in the hallways and Priests no longer taught class. Mary and I both went to the Catholic high school so we were hanging around together a lot. We car pooled to and from school with Stephanie and LeAnn in their little Volkswagon Karmann Ghia; if you can believe that. After school, we hung out with friends.

My parents loved Mary and she went with us often to dinner and shared family vacations. My favorite trip with her family was with her Grandpa and cousins on a houseboat on the river. We water skied, swam and had a blast. Mary was pretty funny and we were always joking around. One evening we were lying on the top of the houseboat and Mary started telling me what every constellation in the sky was named. I was super impressed, until the next day when she told me she was bullshitting me! We did that kind of stuff a lot to each other. We talked about impossible things in public as though we were dead serious, used code words and sayings and confused bystanders and friends alike with our esoteric humor. She had a nickname for me, Shaggy, because of my hair. I called her Scoob in return but not for any other reason than Shaggy and Scoob were inseparable and so were we. We just seemed to "get" each other.

Once again, I was a very loyal friend, perhaps too loyal. Mary was good friends with Sharise, Gina and Emily too. She was someone everyone liked to be around. She was one year older than me therefore she always seemed to pave the way. When I started high school, she had a lot of friends. I didn't really know anyone since I came from the public junior high school across town. I guess I kind of clung to her at the beginning of school. I would wait for her at her locker at break time and we would walk around campus together. One day, Mary wrote me a letter; while it hurt my feelings, it was the straight truth about how she felt and I always appreciated her honesty. She said we were different; she liked to hang out with lots of people and to do lots of things, while I always wanted to just hang out together. She was right. Once again, the fact that I was not really good in crowds stuck out.

I am more of a one on one type person. After "the letter," I started running after school and driving myself to the beach and to the college library to study. I combined my junior and senior year by taking two English classes and two math classes in order to start college early. It wasn't so bad; I didn't mind time to myself. I had friends at school and friends I studied with for class assignments and friends I would do things with on Friday and Saturday nights, but I never really looked for a "best friend" after that letter. I can just hear Mary now, as she reads this book,

"Oh, get over it, Rene!"

Once again, she would be right. I'm really glad she gave me that letter. It made me more self-confident and secure in myself. I realized I had better learn to rely on myself for what I needed; whether it be entertainment or knowing my decisions were what I really wanted out of life. Mary and I stayed BFF's, despite distance and long periods of time without seeing each other. We were maid and matron of honor in each other's weddings, we were pregnant with our second kids at the same time and talked endlessly on the phone about being pregnant and I know she is and always will be there for me and I will be there for her.

A healthy relationship is one in which you understand you are different, you give each other space, you care about each other and support each other and you let the friendship take it's natural course.

Holiday Wishes

When I was growing up, holidays were always different for me from the holidays my friends would describe. Holidays were structured and organized, compared to the free for all commotion my friends would tell me about at their houses. Christmas morning conjures up two images: one, of kids running down to the Christmas tree and ripping open presents and, secondly, of older people sitting around and methodically unwrapping presents. My Christmas mornings were of the second kind. I remember my friends calling me at 8:00 am on Christmas morning, wondering what presents I got for Christmas. They were so excited they could barely get the words out fast enough.

Chrissy would get on the phone first,

"I got a Wonder Woman costume and a Shrinky Dink and a Crissy Doll and a Shaker Maker and Silly String and a Sit 'n Spin and Slime and…"

Next Tim would grab the phone and start spurting out everything he got,

"I got a Magic 8-Ball and a Stretch Armstrong and a G.I. Joe Adventure Team and an Action Jackson and an Atari and a Pet Rock and a Nerf ball and…"

Then Chrissy would grab the phone back,

"And Sharise got a Barbie Corvette and a Barbie Playhouse and an Inchworm and a Lite-Brite and a Weeble and a…. "

They would go on and on and finally stop and say, "What did you get?"

I would have to tell them I hadn't opened presents yet because my parents were still asleep. I had heard stories from Chrissy and Tim that they would jump on their parents' bed to wake them up, sometimes it wasn't even light out yet. In my household, it didn't work that way. My siblings were, themselves, still asleep. My brother may be awake, but my sister was 19 years older than me and fast asleep. Christmas would not only get a slow start at my household, but it would also take forever to complete. My friends would tell wonderful stories of ripping their presents open, all at once, and in a furry. At our house, we opened presents one at a time. After all the adults had sat down on the couch, coffee in hand, someone was chosen to be the present presenter;

"Rene, do you want to hand everyone a present?"

Then, each person would take their moment to slowly unwrap the present, fold the wrapping paper up nicely, place it in the trash bag closest to them, and then upon seeing the present, "ow" and "aw" at what they had received. At which time they would pass it to the person next to them, to ogle and aw and the present would continue to get passed along until everyone had seen it. Opening presents took f-o-r-e-v-e-r. And because we got a late start, I usually wasn't playing with my toys until nearly noon. My friends were so immersed in their games, by the time I showed up, it was hard to break into their play.

I have no idea when this became the custom in my household but it is all I can remember. When my siblings were little, maybe it was wild and crazy. But for me, it was ordered and controlled the entire time I was growing up. I assume this is due to the fact I was so much younger than everyone else. My sisters were 19 and 16 years older and my brother was 8 years older. That means when I was 9 and excited, I was alone. My brother was already 17 and mellow and my sisters were 28 and 25. Even the "aftermath" of Christmas was nice and tidy and looked nothing like I saw at other houses. Our treasures were neatly stacked on a couch cushion and trash was immediately taken out. What I saw at other homes looked like a tornado had hit the living room; wrapping paper, bows, ribbons and toys were everywhere. It looked incredibly fun!

Even though I moved away for college, I always went home for Christmas. My "then-boyfriend," Seth, on his first Christmas with us, was baffled. I don't think he had ever imagined Christmas morning so well practiced. We were like a well-oiled machine with instructions on how to operate. He was sweet though and never complained; he learned the routine and fit right in. On the other hand, my first Christmas with Seth's family was exciting for me. We were married and his older sister and her husband already had a baby. I had to make myself go out of turn and just grab a present like everyone else. It was total mayhem and these were 20 year olds! Wrapping paper was flying and the mound of presents under the tree was disappearing as though it were running water. It was a little chaotic after so many years of doing it my family's way. I didn't really get to see any of the other presents and it was over so fast. In the end it was a bit disappointing to have built up so much anticipation for an event I prepared all month for, only to have it last a few moments. I guess familiarity becomes comfortable and, after so many years, what I thought I had wanted became odd. A couple of years down the line, when we had kids of our own, we opted for a Christmas morning somewhere in the middle. We wake up as early as the kids want, but we grab our coffee that was made early on a timer. Our kids grab presents for themselves, but they also enjoy handing them out to Mama and Papa, since we only have a few. They love to rip open the wrapping, ball it up and throw it into a giant pile. The entire living room floor is covered in goodies and toys are piled around their bodies. Shortly after, they gang up with their cousins and hang out for the rest of the morning playing with their treasures. I make Christmas Eve dinner for everyone and so on Christmas day I get to relax and enjoy the excitement. My dear Mama makes Christmas dinner. Christmas morning is my favorite morning of the year; it always has been, whether slow and methodical or fun and easy, the spirit of Christmas will always be present.

Birthday celebrations for me were also mature events that mainly included expensive dinners and one nice gift. I spent every birthday growing up going to the restaurant of my choice with my family. While my friends often had birthday parties, my parents seemed so happy to go to dinner on my birthday with me that I never asked to change it up. My parents felt like birthdays were family events more than friend events. My Papa would love to talk about the day I was born and the day felt more like a shared day than just my day. This may be because he was older and cherished the day and didn't want to share it with passing friends or maybe it was just his way. I was the baby and he and my mom held on to me tightly. Upon turning 13, I did divert and beg my parents for a birthday beach party. My birthday fell in early September, which at the time was before school started. I called around and invited as many friends as I could get a hold of on the phone. Too bad I didn't have texting back then! I invited a bunch of kids and they were to meet at my house and then my parents were going to pack us up and take us to the beach. About 45 minutes after the meeting time of 9am, it became apparent most kids were no shows. I must have looked pretty pathetic sitting and waiting for kids who weren't showing up. The final straw for my Dad was when Lisa showed up but her twin sister didn't make it because she wasn't feeling well. With only a few kids present, my Dad announced we instead were going to Disneyland! When Lisa called her Mom to ask if it were alright, her sister Laura all of a sudden felt great and asked if she could go too. I will always remember feeling relieved when my Dad played the bad guy and said, "No, sorry but your sister is sick, remember?" My feelings were so hurt that no one showed up and my Dad was my hero for saving the day and making my birthday great. I was lucky he could afford to take us all. There are two big advantages to having older parents; they have money and are observant. They know the ways of kids and how to get back at childish bad behavior. My Dad could tell kids were flaking for no real reason and believe me, a ton of kids came to me later that week at school and said how bummed they were that they didn't get to go to Disneyland and how cool it was that my parents took us. My Mom and Dad took what was a horrifying experience and turned it into a good memory. At their age, they were wise and seemed to be able to save the day more than once. I still have a fear when throwing a party though; I guess you never forget those childhood disastrous moments.

Grandparents

Like holidays, my family get-togethers were different from my friends. The biggest difference was I didn't spend much time with my grandparents. One reason being, three out of four of my grandparents had passed away from old age. By the time I was old enough to understand family dynamics, my one old grandma didn't really have the energy for me. I was the number 25th grandchild from her four children. By me, she had held enough babies, kissed enough toddlers and talked to enough five year olds. She wasn't really interested in me. She was intimidating and I can recall the handful of moments with her. It wasn't always like that. My siblings recall family parties with 24 children running around and having a blast. They were Catholic, so there were a lot of kids and a lot of First Communion parties. But my cousins were all grown up by my birth. Life was quiet at my house. I didn't see my cousins except when I was really, really young. I remember a few family parties. My cousins were older and usually watching scary movies, like Carrie, or talking about mature subjects, like sex and drugs. The only thing they said to me was,

"Go find your Mommy."

I never met my Mom's dad; he was hit by a truck before I was born. I do remember my Mama's Mother staying with us once when I was 5 and I had the Chicken Pox. She was really sweet and I wish I could have spent more time with her. My Mama always said her mother was an angel and from the stories I have heard, it sounds correct. She seemed like that perfect grandma; round and sweet, and I bet she was good at rocking and singing lullabies. She knew a lot of old stories and tales; my parents recorded her telling these stories and I have heard the recordings but I don't remember her telling them unfortunately.

I'm proud of my female lineage; I come from good, strong women. My Mama's Mom was a very hard worker and kept her family afloat during "The Depression." She was the caretaker and provider of my Mama's childhood memories and I think it is her strength I see living on in my Mama. My Grandma grew up on a farm in Kansas at the turn of the century and when she was young she became a teacher; one of two professions offered to women during that time period. When there were no jobs in the 1920's, she washed and ironed clothes and linens for the wealthy people in town. She did what needed to be done to keep her family fed and housed and I look inside myself to find her spirit when I feel weak. My mother also has spirit and is determined in her actions. She sticks to her beliefs and lives according to her values.

I have a family secret. I never knew this until recently, but my Mom was a virgin until she met my Dad. Well, she doesn't know it, but I was too. And now that my daughter is older, she waited until she fell head over heels in love also. It's funny to find something like that got passed on even when no one knew they were passing it on.

I remember talking to my father's Dad briefly once in the kitchen; he was wearing grey mechanic overalls and I was hungry. He walked over to the kitchen counter and pulled off a brown banana from the bunch and handed it to me. When I made a face he said, "the brown ones are the best, don't complain." He became very ill when I was 10. I visited him when he was bedbound and it was very sad. I remember his face being thin and his facial hair was stubbly. I kind of backed away when my Dad took me near him because I was scared. My Dad remembered that moment very well and it later impacted decisions he made for himself. The next time I saw my Grandpa was at his bedside as he died. I can't recall his character. He was an old man to me and I wish I could say more about him. It makes me sad I'm not able to recall who he was as a person.

So, as it turns out, it is my Dad's Mom, my grandmother, who I remember best. She held me on her lap once when I was 4, while I looked at her necklace, and then she bought me a necklace just like hers; I still have it. She went with us to Lake Havasu once and while we were there she told me a story about growing up in the Canadian forest with 12 siblings. Her mother died when she was a baby and her father had to eventually send her and her sisters to a girl's catholic convent to be raised. What an incredible childhood; so different from mine. When I was 5, my brother and I stayed with her and my grandpa for New Year's Eve; I don't remember seeing my Grandpa, but I do remember her putting us to bed on the couch at 8pm. They had an old ranch house in La Habra Heights and we could see clear to Catalina Island from their living room. Late that night my brother and I watched the fireworks in the sky over Disneyland. It was beautiful, but a little bit eerie. My Grandmother was asleep in her room and my Grandfather was asleep in his room.

When I was 12 I went with my Aunt and Uncle to Tahoe. My grandmother was with us and my older cousins. It was my first time to go snow skiing. On our way to the mountains we stopped in a restaurant to eat. I will always remember what happened next and it is how I will think of my Grandmother and her nature forever more. She and I were walking to the restroom and had to pass by the bar area. She was 83 and I was 13 but I looked 18, as far as boobs and height were concerned. I didn't notice anything as we walked but when we got back to the table my Grandmother said to my relatives:

"You should have seen those men at the bar when we walked by them! They were staring at my legs and flirting with me!"

She had a confidence beyond most.

My Grandmother was at my wedding, she held my first baby and then I didn't see her again until she was dying. I took my two year old and drove to Lake Havasu where she lived. She was deaf and by the time I arrived, she wasn't very coherent. I tried to talk with her but how do you share such a personal moment with someone you should know really well, but don't? I never saw her again. I missed her funeral and I missed saying goodbye.

That is the extent of my grandparent memories. There was a space in my heart that seemed to be reserved for grandparents that never got filled. It made me want my own children to spend a lot of time with their grandparents. I realized early on with the age of my parents, it would take a lot of concerted effort to make that happen.

"You are your Papa's Daughter!"

My first memory is probably not my own. I have heard stories told for so long that most likely I created images matching the story I heard. Either way, I swear I remember looking out of my eyes, across the room to my sister by the door and then I see images of falling forward toward the ground. As if in slow motion, I see the twin bed to my right and the edge of the desk underneath my baby seat. As I fall, I see the ground below me, coming toward me. Then my memory ends. This is my first memory in life. I was 3 months old.

If events form our expectations, you would think I would be afraid of heights and I would have a hard time trusting my sister. Neither is true. In fact, my sister is extremely trustworthy and I am not the least bit afraid of heights; jumping out of a plane at 5000 feet high was one of the most exhilarating events of my life. So, I am left asking, "Why? Why do I remember that event? Why do I remember any event over another for that matter? Certain events in our life are forged into our brain like a sculptor hammers his chisel into rock. These random events sculpt us, unbeknown to us.

My first years were full of adventures; sprained wrists, stitches and scars were all a part of me by the time I was 6 years old. At 2, I rode a plastic Snoopy toy down a steep hill, only to wipe out in front of a neighbor's driveway. At 3, I dropped a steel rebar on my foot, smashing and destroying my big toe which is still deformed. Later that year, I wrestled my brother until he flipped me over his back, splitting my chin on the tile and sending me to the emergency room. At 4, I climbed a wall to get on my brother's yellow, Schwinn ten speed bike and couldn't quite reach the pedals to make it go all the way around it's rotation without kicking it around. I rode it for a while and then realized I had to fall over to get off. Scraped knees and elbows were a part of my daily routine. I was definitely a tom boy. The summer I turned 5, I learned how to water-ski on the Colorado River. I also was crazy enough to climb to the very top of Jumping Rock at Lake Havasu and jump from the top of the cliff. I remember talking to some college boys standing at the cliffs edge before I jumped but I was too young to realize I had thoroughly shamed them because they had been standing there for 10 minutes, afraid themselves to jump. When I got to the boat, my Papa told me what I had done to those boys and I still didn't really get it. I jumped off that rock all summer long so I didn't think it was any big deal. At 6, I accidentally broke a carnival oil lamp on my wrist, cutting my wrist vein and causing profuse bleeding that actually squirted across the room. When I ran downstairs to my Mama, she was on the phone. I was holding my wrist with blood everywhere. Most parents would have panicked, but not my Mama. She simply told her friend she needed to get off the phone; she hung up and wrapped a towel around my wrist. My brother went to the emergency room with us and I can still picture him fainting and falling off the high stool when they started to stitch me up.

There wasn't anything I wouldn't try or was scared to try. I drove and docked our boat with no reverse, drove our Jeep with roll bars up mountains and I created adventures for myself as often as possible. I would disappear into the hills for the entire day, hiking around by myself; climbing into coyote dens, catching snakes, swimming in muddy creeks and climbing through underground sewer pipes. I was a young girl growing up on the outskirts of a big city and I witnessed a lot. I was chased and shot by a boy with a pellet gun. Fortunately, instead of being hit in the tummy, my pants metal snap stopped the pellet. Once, during a football game at the college, I was tricked into the forest by a boy who tried to hurt me; he said his little brother was lost in the forest and since I knew the forest so well, I tried to help, instead when I realized what was happening, I stepped on his toe as hard as I could and ran. I was followed twice by men using cameras to take pictures of me, once on the beach and once on the city street; both times a person warned me and I ran away.

I rode my bike, hiked and walked all over my little suburban town. When I got into high school, I would ride my bike west on the L.A. aqueduct to the Pacific Ocean, turn south onto PCH and ride past Beer Can Beach to Huntington Beach and then turn east and ride home on Beach Blvd.; arriving way after dark. At 14 years old, my friends, Mary, Sharise, Emily, Gina and I started going to concerts in Hollywood, limo rides to Santa Monica Beach, shopping on Melrose Avenue, walks down Skid Row and dancing at The Palace: every day events in the life of a teenager growing up around L.A. Perhaps, learning I could survive a three foot fall at 3 months old led me to believe I could survive anything thrown my way. I continued to look for adventure and to try what others' would not try.

My parents were like other parents in the 70's; "be home before dark," was all they said. Often I would come home, way after the street lamps had turned on, to find my mom mad and my dinner cold. But we kids were not shuttled around from play date to play date back then and so after an angry word with a sharp tone in my mother's voice, we moved on. My parents were attentive, but the world is cruel and they wanted to raise me to be tough enough to manage in it. After three children before me, they weren't afraid of me getting hurt; they were more concerned with me being tough.

My Papa didn't know if he would always be around for me and prepped me to be mature and able to take care of myself. He talked to me as though I were an adult. He asked me heavy questions and expected thoughtful answers. He told me about the world; the good and the bad. I noticed he turned every discussion into a lesson. He was the consummate teacher and I, his pupil.

When other kids threw eggs at houses for fun, my mind questioned the damage of the egg on the paint of the house and the money it would cost the owners to repaint that area. My conscience was tuned like a grand piano to resonate any movement around me. Guilt is not only a Catholic privilege; it is also a consequence of thought. My Papa stressed the importance of responsibility,

"Take responsibility for your life, for your actions, for your decisions and for the people around you."

He learned responsibility as an officer in the Navy. I learned responsibility as his daughter. He didn't push me specifically; he just let it be known there are consequences for all decisions and to not make a decision is a decision in and of itself. So I decided to take responsibility for my life and I left for college at age 16. Time was always of the essence and never could I afford to waste time. My Mama was sad to see me leave, but my Papa was relieved he had lived long enough to see me go. They were in their 60's when I left.

The night before I left for college, I cried myself to sleep, as I had done for many years. I cried because my parents were old. I was leaving them and I was afraid of what the future held; would they grow older faster while I was gone? I had already lost both Grandpas and my one Grandma. My Dad's sister was ill with cancer and I was worried my parents were next. I had a great childhood, but it was time for me to grow up. Not because it was "my time" to grow up, but because it was their time for me to be a grown up. It was time for me to grow up and relieve my parents of their responsibility for me. They were too old to worry about me. And they were too old for me to stick around, acting like a kid. I needed to move on so they could act their age.

Chapter 3

Second Life Stage: Awakening

Long Distance Relationship

I still had braces on my teeth, the day my family dropped me off at my dorm room. I was 16 years old. I had a single room because I wanted privacy and it was scary to think about having a roommate that could be 19 years old. At first, the day was busy. I had to wait in line to get my key, find my room, unload the car, set up the microwave, refrigerator and (there were no computers back then) hang my clothes. After my Papa helped me build shelving, my family was ready to leave.

I walked my Mama, Papa, brother and sister out to the car. They all got in after saying their goodbyes. My Papa backed the car out of the parking space and drove away. I couldn't see through the tinted windows, but I waved as they left. The day was sunny, the sky was blue, a seagull flew overhead and it was silent in my world. My Mama says she will never forget that moment. She was leaving her baby girl. As she turned her head to watch me wave goodbye, she could see tears on my cheek. She says her heart broke and the sadness that she wouldn't see me but for a couple of times a year crept into her and seeded itself there forever more. When it comes to watching your baby move out of the house, age doesn't matter. A new chapter in life, for both daughter and Mama, child and parent, had begun.

College life was fun. I enjoyed my classes and I loved living on my own. I didn't have a phone and cell phones didn't exist. I wrote a few letters home, but my mind was far away from my childhood and home. I liked the freedom; the time to myself. I rode my bike every day for hours through the beautiful neighborhoods and up into the mountains that rose from sea level to 6800 feet. 'I went to parties and joined the water ski team. Although I went home for Christmas, I made sure to plan a camping trip to the Grand Canyon for Spring break. I wasn't lonely and I didn't realize I had left my Mama and Papa alone after 36 years of having children in the house, to face each other and their relationship. Marriage dynamics were the last thing on my mind. I didn't think much about my parents and what their life had become. My first year in college was about me. It was the only year of my life, so far, that was only about me.

At 17, I met my future husband, Seth, and I have been forever grateful and happy to share my life with him. He and I had so much fun in college. We surfed up and down the coast of California; spending many nights in his van on the side of the road until the sun started to rise and we could see the surf. Then out into the ocean we would paddle. We studied and did well in school, but our main focus was enjoying life. We were always together from the moment we met and at 20, we were married. Inspired by Ruth Benedict's statement, "The purpose of anthropology is to make the world safe for human differences," I entered the Ph.D. program in Anthropology. The next summer we went to Bali, Indonesia for two months to study and surf. We were good kids; we went home to my parent's house for every birthday and holiday. Seth really got to know my parents well. After I graduated with my Master's degree in Anthropology, Seth and I had our daughter, Kai, and I decided to drop out of the Ph.D. program to raise Kai full time. I loved being a young Mom. Kai was incredibly happy and sweet. Seth and I were able to travel to Bali with her for a couple of months when she was one year old and we all had an amazing time. Life was wonderful. We worked at an organic farm, saw family a lot and enjoyed driving around in our van, surfing and camping up and down the coast.

When Seth graduated with his degree in Geography we decided to move to Hawaii. We were 26 years old. The move went well and Seth found a job soon enough. He worked at home on his computer and Kai and I kept him company. We would take turns surfing at V-land and Kai loved playing in the warm Pacific Ocean. It was when the holidays started to roll around that we realized my parents didn't even have a plane ticket reserved to come visit us. Kai had spent so much time with her grandparents up until the age of 3, but she would soon forget them and never get to know them if they didn't come visit. We could see into the future and see that we would maybe see my parents once every couple of years. I had watched my older sister move to Oregon and I saw her only a handful of times while I was growing up. She was 16 years older than me. My Mom and Dad were busy parenting me and we never really got to visit her. On the other hand, she was too busy working and paying bills to come down to California for visits. So, from past experiences, I could see how this was going to play out. That's when Seth and I decided we were Californians, through and true; our families lived in California and the earth of the California coast had been our home for generations. We could tell a long distance, family relationship wouldn't work for us; our kids would never get to know their grandparents and cousins and that seemed too sad for us. So, we moved back to California.

Raising a Family

We moved back, found a cute little cottage in Montecito and Seth found a job. When we moved to Silver Strand in Oxnard we were only one hour from my parents and saw them often. My parents were in their 70's and they were really enjoying life. After I went to college, they started travelling on cruise ships. My Papa had been a navigator in the Navy therefore to cruise around the world was perfect for him. They went to every continent and travelled through most countries. They circumnavigated the globe twice and climbed high into Tibet and Peru. They were so busy travelling, once we went down and decorated their entire house for Christmas. They were cutting it so close to the holiday that they were barely back in time to celebrate.

After a year in an office cubicle atmosphere, Seth struck out on his own. He had grown up in a little town along California's Central Coast. It was a great town but there were very few jobs. The day his own company brought in a nice large paycheck we drove to his hometown and found a house. Kai started kindergarten and I started helping Seth. A year later I gave birth to our son. He was such a happy baby boy.

He loved his big sister and Seth and I were so lucky to be able to be at home with them both every day. We spent many hours going to the beach and swimming at the park. Seth worked very hard and it was a very busy time. But we would find hours here and there to sip coffee in the sun, hike to remote surf spots, and drive our inflatable boat up the coast to surf spots not accessible by vehicle.

My parents came up often, mainly because we had a nice big house and room for guests. Life was good. They really liked the Central Coast and my Papa felt it was time for them to be closer to family. They were 78 years old and not getting any younger. In 2002, my parents sold their home of 38 years, the home I was born in and married in, and moved to the Central Coast. I moved them into their new home on our 13th Anniversary. My husband gave up the day and has given me up on many other days since. It was really nice having Grandma and Grandpa around. Our son was 4 years old, our daughter was 10, and the kids loved having their grandparents in town. By then we had a 4000 square foot house and so I took on most of the holiday dinners. What a dream; 20 people whom I loved, sitting around our dining room table. Seth's Mom lived with us, off and on, and his sister with her family also lived in town. Everything was wonderful.

Those were magical years when I had everything I ever wanted. Life was still sticky and difficult; like life is, but I was surrounded in love while raising our family.

My Dream

When Seth and I were living in Hawaii and it struck us our children would never see their relatives, we moved back to California. It was so important to us that our children have a close connection to their grandparents. I felt strongly about this, I guess, because I always pictured the perfect childhood including the sweet chubby grandma who would bake cookies and color in coloring books with her grandchildren. Children grow up so fast. Had Seth and I not moved back from Hawaii, our children would have grown up without the memories they now share with their Grandma and Grandpa. We now look back on countless sweet memories of Grandma coloring with Kai and Grandpa sitting with his grandson on his lap with the both of them falling asleep, Grandma playing Legos with her little grandson and Grandpa having endless conversations with Kai about her dreams and aspirations. It took a lot of effort from both families to bring us all together. Sure Seth and I moved from Hawaii to California, but my parents uprooted their entire life from what they had known, to move to be with us.

My parents were raised in Compton and Lynwood, California, in the 1920's and 1930's. Their entire lives were spent in Los Angeles. They were married and raised their children there. I was born in the same house I got married in. They had all their memories and friends in Southern California and they left it for us. That kind of family dedication is priceless and meant the absolute world to me. I had never realized how much I missed my parents until I was living in the same town again with them.

My husband and I struck out at a young age, 20 years old, to prove we could make it on our own. We have been a team through thick and thin. There is no one in this world I trust more to have my back. I love him more than life itself and I would jump out of a plane after him to give him my parachute. When my parents moved to town and I was reminded of how much they cared for me and loved me and my family, life somehow felt whole. I didn't know what I was missing until I found my completeness again. I had ditched my parents when I went to college. I only did what was expected of every strong, intelligent, hard-working young adult and that is to start a life of one's own. But now that I had created this life of mine, it felt good to have my parent's become a part of it.

When my parents moved at the age of 78, I didn't realize how old they were already. They were in such great shape and their mental acuteness was so sharp. They had been old my entire life, so this was just another stage of "old." I knew how lucky I was to not only have them with me, but to have the opportunity to spend so much time with them. My career in real estate allowed me the opportunity to go out to lunch with them a couple of times a week or even drop by their house while I was driving around for Thursday caravan. We spent every holiday together without the stress of travel and the children became close to their grandparents. We lived only minutes away from each other and were able to see each other whenever we wanted. That freedom is worth all the money in the world. I will always cherish the memories and times we shared together as one, big, happy family. And I am so glad all of us put effort into making it happen.

Chapter 4

Third Life Stage: Awareness

Paris

The summer of 2009 was my most lucrative summer as a Realtor. I had been a Realtor for 6 years and was really hitting my stride. My husband and I finally had our finances manageable; we had no credit debt, our vehicles were paid off and, although we were not swimming in dough, we were able to buy the kids what they needed. We were 40 years old. Life was simple and sweet.

My parents had lived on the Central Coast for 7 years by 2009. They had become so busy and comfortable. Our town is a population of only about 5000 people and they knew half of them in no time. They had met a whole different group of people than I knew and had made so many wonderful friends. They were involved in a lot of group activities and went to a ton of events. One night, they came over after the Oktoberfest and told us they had won the grand prize; they had won a trip to Germany for two. It was pretty exciting.

While they were really social, they were never too social to miss our Friday lunch every week. They most often would pick me up at my office downtown on Main Street. My parents would walk into my office and usually enjoy a conversation or two while I wrapped things up. We would then walk across the street to our favorite restaurant, Old Stone Station. The owner, Carl, and the waiter, Jay, are fantastic and treated my parents like locals love to be treated; they knew what we liked, how we liked it and they were always so sweet as to give us the 10% local discount. The other place we would go to eat lunch on Fridays is The Hamlet. This is a restaurant on Highway 1 (we don't call it PCH up here) and the grounds and views are amazing! Lucy was the best waitress ever and my parents loved her because they had all been dancers in the local Follies production. My parents were always the most fantastic Swing dancers on the floor; people would part, sit down and watch when my parents hit the dance floor. Take into account this is even when they were in their 80's! So anyway, one day we are on our way to the Hamlet for lunch. I am in the back seat of my parents Tahoe and my Papa asks me this question,

"Love, if you could have anything, what would it be?"

"Papa, I have everything I need."

"But, if you could do something or have something, what would it be?"

"O.k., it would be to have you forever! There, that's what I want. I want you and Mama with me for 30 more years! I know you said you'd be with me until my 50th birthday, but I want you for longer!"

Remember, I was in the back seat. So, I couldn't see my Papa's eyes, but I can imagine after hearing my request for him to live 30 more years, his heart must have been breaking and his eyes welling up with tears.

"Well, I don't know about that, but your Mama and I are going to send you and Seth to Europe for your 20th Wedding Anniversary!"

Wow! My parents were giving Seth and I the Oktoberfest prize they had won. Something inside of me said I best set the trip up fast. So I called Seth and asked if he could take two weeks off at the end of the month. He called his boss and we set the trip up for two weeks away.

Instead of Germany, we planned a trip to Paris and London. My Papa really wanted us to experience Paris; no wonder why! Paris was absolutely beautiful! Seth and I hadn't been on a vacation in so many years, let alone, had time to ourselves. We had the best time ever. We saw a symphony at the Old Paris Opera House, we saw the opera, Salome, at the new Bastille Opera House, we spent a day in the Louvre, and visited countless other museums. We stopped in every café we passed by and had either an espresso or a Stella Artoise, depending on our mood. We walked nearly 20 miles a day. We relaxed and laughed and completely enjoyed ourselves. Thank you, Mama and Papa, for giving us a trip of a lifetime and for taking care of the kids while we were gone.

While we were in Paris, there was a silent acknowledgement that this gift, this trip, was more special than just a generous offering. I had a feeling my Papa was sick and life was about to change. I mentioned this to our friends in England. Hearing the words come out of my mouth solidified the enormity of the moment. My Papa was not just sending us to Europe, he was watching us enjoy ourselves one last time; giving us a memory for the rest of our life. It was a testament of my parents' love for us.

Thanksgiving

When we came home from Paris, my Papa and Mama came by the house in their truck. They didn't get out, but my Mama said from the driver's side window that they just wanted to see us. My Papa sat in the passenger seat. He wasn't feeling well and didn't want to get us sick, but when I looked into his eyes I knew my suspicions were confirmed. My Papa was not feeling well, but something far worse than the flu was hurting him. They drove away that day, without a word spoken, but my sadness was seeping into every cell of my being. I knew when we were in Paris and London something was wrong. I didn't know what, but I could tell. My Papa wanted to see us have fun and have an adventure. Thank you, Mama and Papa, for sending me around the world. Thank you for giving me two weeks of pure enjoyment and relaxation. Those days have carried me through the years. I can't say, "poor me," because you have always given me so much.

The next day, I went to work. I met with my Broker in the back room. I said to him,

"My Papa is very sick. I don't know what it is yet, he hasn't told me, but I know it is something really bad. I want to let you know I probably won't be coming to work anymore. I don't know what's going to happen, but I will be helping my parents as much as they need and for as long as they need it."

I actually was not that fluid or eloquent because I think I was crying the entire time I was talking. He understood and said that was fine, "take as much time as you need."

We came home from Paris in mid-November. On Thanksgiving night, my table was set, we were all gathered around and my Papa said the prayer. I saw my Papa cry once; it was at my Grandpa's bedside as my Grandpa died. Thanksgiving night, I saw my Papa shed one tear and never did I see him cry again. He was so strong. He said a beautiful prayer and thanked God for giving him such a beautiful and wonderful wife. He said he had had such a wonderful life and was very thankful for everything and especially everyone God had given him. I can't remember all of the words verbatim, but I do remember glancing around the table and seeing my sisters with the saddest look on their faces and with the reddest eyes, I remember watching my Mama trying to stay so composed. The absolute sadness that draped itself over the people around that table is hauntingly beautiful. That we loved each other so much, that we could share such an impacting moment, that we entered into sadness together, is the gift of life. We were not alone. My Papa was not alone. He was surrounded by his family; the family he grew, the family he loved more than anything on this earth. No specifics were mentioned, we just all knew life was about to change.

My papa was sitting in his favorite chair in my living room. He took my arm gently, pulled me near and said,

"Love, I want you to take good care of your Mama. Can you do that for me?"

"Of course, Papa, of course I will."

I relive that moment every day. I made a promise to my Papa that I will keep. Nobody knows he said that to me; not even my Mama. My siblings are all older than I am and sometimes they wonder why I am in charge. It's because of the relationship my Papa and I had together. I understood his dedication to my Mama and I promised my Papa I would continue to help her live the way he intended. I may fail in many areas of life, but being loyal to my family is the one thing in this world I do without falter. I am a good caretaker. My Papa knew this and it was the reason he moved himself and my Mama to be close to me as they grew old.

The Saturday after Thanksgiving we all gathered at my parent's home. We sat in the living room; my Papa in his Eames style chair. We all knew what we were there for; my Papa was going to tell us what was wrong. He placed his left hand over the right side of his chest and said he had lung cancer and the cancer was the size of a tennis ball.

"I came into this world with no scars and I will leave with no scars."

My Papa chose to not go to the hospital. He chose to not have treatments. He chose to stay at home, where he was most comfortable, with the people he loved. He and my Mama explained to us the living will and the family trust they had been busily setting up. Fortunately for all of us, my Papa was given a warning of what was to come. He had time to prepare.

A Rare, Special Moment

My daughter, Kai, was very close to her grandfather. My Dad was fascinated by her artistic talent and loved to hear her opinions. He read stories she wrote and always wanted to know about her classes at school. He thirsted for knowledge and inspired my children to crave that same intellectual stimulation. My daughter has a memory that happens very rarely; an opportunity to share something with someone so special that it carries a power of its own. When my daughter applied to college, she applied to one college and for early admittance. At age 9 she determined for herself that she would attend California Polytechnic State University, as an Architect major. She worked very hard through-out her Junior High and High School career to achieve that goal. When the time came to apply to colleges, she knew what she wanted and she wouldn't compromise. She applied only to California Polytechnic.

My Dad got sick in October and died in March. College applicants don't find out if they are accepted to colleges until April or so; unless they apply for early acceptance and then it is a risk because fewer are chosen. Had Kai applied regular decision, this story would not be told. But she didn't and this is the story she shares now with her Grandpa:

My Papa was still strong enough to walk up the stairs, but he wasn't leaving the house. I was visiting with Papa one day in his living room when I got a call from Seth.

"Kai's letter from California Polytechnic is here! What should I do?"

"Oh, hi sweetie…."

"I can't tell what it says, but I held it up to the light and I think I can make out the word, "congratulations," but I'm not sure. It's in a regular size envelope, which usually is a denial… Kai's down stairs. I should send her over there with you and your Dad to open the letter…."

"Are you sure, Sweetie? That would be so incredibly unselfish of you. This is a big deal for you too!"

"I know, but it would be really special for your Dad to be there with Kai when she opens it. I'll give her some papers and tell her you need them for work."

"Wow. I really love you a lot."

"I'll send her over right now."

Kai drove over to my parents' home, delivering what she thought were real estate papers I needed. When she came into the living room, she sat down next to Grandpa and gave him a big hug.

"I love you Grandpa. How do you feel?"

"Pretty good, little one. How are you?"

"I'm well, Grandpa."

"Mama, Papa gave me these papers for you."

"Oh, thank you, Kai. But I think there is something there for you too!"

"Oh?"

With that, Kai found her letter from California Polytechnic. Her hands started shaking and she looked at Grandpa and me with wide eyes. She was very nervous and it showed.

"Oh my God, Mama! It's here. I'm scared."

"It'll be o.k. sweetie. Go ahead. Open it."

Kai was sitting in between her Grandpa and me. She looked at the envelope, inspected it and then slowly began opening it. When the single piece of paper had been removed and unfolded, her hands were shaking so much she could hardly read the words.

"We are pleased to inform you your application to California Polytechnic State University has been accepted. Congratulations, you have been admitted into the Department of Architecture for fall quarter, 2010."

Tears of absolute joy streamed down Kai's and my face. We stood up and hugged. She was shaking she was so happy.

Months of unknowing…years of preparation… moments of joy….

Grandpa looked on.

This was a moment he knew could not be beat for years to come. Perhaps not until graduation would Mama be prouder, perhaps not until her wedding day would Kai be happier, perhaps not until the day of her first child's birth would tears flow so freely…these are the moments in life that are few and far between. These are the moments Grandpa knew he would no longer share with us, beyond this moment.

…Beyond this moment.

The Human Spirit is Amazing

I am not a doctor, but I had to help care for my Papa until he died. I am not a lawyer, but I had to help make sure all the "paperwork" was in order. I am not a psychologist, but I had to help counsel my Mama when she thought she couldn't go on. When I look back on the six months my Mom, my sister and I spent taking care of my Papa, at home, while he lay dying of lung cancer, I am humbled. The human spirit is beyond my understanding. How were we strong enough? How did I tell my Papa it was o.k. for him to leave us? Why on earth, did I think I could become him and take care of everything? I never hesitated. I did what I needed to do. I contribute this to my Papa. He never hesitated. He never showed any fear of dying. He was amazing throughout his life and death. I was so strong in front of him. Now, I just need to stay strong. How did he do it? Does strength like his come innately from inside? Was it programmed into his brain? Did he ever question himself inside his head? The only thing I have come to know and rely on as true is this; when the time comes for me to be strong and to make a decision, the strength is and will be there. When I am by myself, at my desk, fixing old tax mistakes or calling insurance companies or making doctor appointments or paying bills or something else frightening and/or tedious, I wonder where I will find the strength. I cry sometimes when I am alone. It is better to let it out than to hold it in. When my Mama tells me she feels bad because I have to do everything for her, I honestly and truthfully tell her,

"It's ok Mama. I love being with you. I love helping you with everything and hanging out all the time. I wouldn't want it any other way. I love you so much. You took such good care of me all the time I was young. Now I get to help you and I appreciate being able to be with you!"

I know I am happy and if I relax, everything will be ok. I don't pray like I did when I was a little girl. I no longer beg, bargain and ask favors. But I do pray. I throw my thoughts out into the universe. I ask God to watch over my family and to keep them safe and healthy and happy. I do believe in, "ask and you shall receive." I think it means the same as, "create your own reality." I believe the trick is to trust yourself and know in your heart as long as you do your best for the people you love and have in your life, then your mind will rest at ease. Life is not always fun or easy; it is only fun and easy once in a while and that is why we appreciate those moments. But life can be good. We cannot control people and events in our life, but we can appreciate the beauty of each hug and of each smile from the people in our life. I tell myself, "The human spirit is amazing; know this, rest assured of this and realize what you need to do will be revealed when needed."

I tell myself this, I trust myself and then I move on.

Papa's Memorial

"A couple of days after my Papa died, I wrote down some words.

Not in an attempt to give a synopsis of my Dad's life; who he was or what he believed in. They were simply thoughts that have helped me during this time.

So if you'll bear with me:

My Papa was a teacher.

Although he liked to speak more than most, it was not through his words that he taught me the most about life.

He taught me the most through the choices he made throughout his exemplary living.

My Dad believed that all there are in this life are choices.

My Dad chose how to live…and how to die.

I have never met anyone as confident as him in his choices.

He was always so assured of himself.

He is the strongest person I will ever know.

Thank you, Papa , for showing me how to be strong.

He is also the most truthful person I will ever know.

He never side stepped the truth, but instead faced it head on.

He always was willing to tell the truth, no matter how hard.

And I greatly respect him for that.

Thank you, Papa, for teaching me the importance of truth.

One point my Dad liked to make is this:

'There are no problems in this world, only solutions.'

My Papa was a problem solver.

Even in his dying, he chose how to solve that one last problem in life, "How was he going to die?"

He died as he lived; strong, truthful and making his own choices.

Thank you, Papa, for teaching me these things. Thank you for teaching me through your life and death about strength and the truth of life.

I would like to now introduce the Honor Guard from the American Legion and the California National Guard.

The California National Guard will be doing the flag folding and will present the flag, in honor of Carl.

Please stand for Taps and be seated once it is over.

Part II

Chapter 5

Fourth Life Stage: Knowing

Papa lived through the winter, only to die in March. But it was as though he left us in our own winter for years to come.

Six months after my Papa died, my daughter started college and my son was having fun in junior high. I thoroughly enjoyed watching my children continue to grow. I was a 100% participant in my relationship with my husband, my kids and my Mama. But I didn't have the time or energy for anyone else.

Nine months after my Papa died, I tried to go back to work but I could not focus on the needs of clients when I was needed so much at home. My Mama needed me every day for many reasons, some reasons were very serious. She and I were in a state of transition. It was important I acknowledged I needed time to heal. I realized that to push my pain down deep inside would only be a way of hiding and ignoring the pain instead of dealing with it. So I didn't commit to anyone at work, which is very easy to do in real estate. I had transitioned all my clients away from me when my Papa got sick and I just never called or asked for them to come back.

I wake up in the morning and the day seems so different. Life has changed and the changes are apparent. Hours feel like days and days feel like weeks. Weeks feel like months and then I lose track of time completely and a week goes by and it is the same every day, so a week feels like a day. And then a year goes by and I swear it was just a few months ago you died. And then one day, I have been reliving the day after your death for two years and I try to change, but I can't. I'm pulled into this vortex and everyone changes around me, but I am stuck in this one place.

For two years, every day felt like the day after my Papa died. My Mama was "doing as well as could be expected," as she would say, but after 62 years of marriage...what can I say? That is her story to tell. I would wake up, take care of my family and then spend most days with my Mama. Holidays, and every day, were warm and loving, but we could always feel the absence of my Papa.

Three years down the road, life is understandable and feeling normal again, for me, but not for my Mama. She is well and is involved, but her soul mate, her life companion, her Captain, is gone. And every day, for her, feels like the first day without Carl.

Mortality and Old Age

I come home after my Mama's doctor appointment and I am feeling exhausted. I wasn't gone for many hours, I didn't travel for a long distance, but mentally, I'm drained. These are new experiences for me; thinking about my Mama's health and being her partner in making health decisions. It's important I think and consider everything involved in order to help her make the right decisions. I am inexperienced, but learning fast. Geriatric medicine is something I didn't give a lot of thought toward, until now. I am not special or different; I know friends who have lost their Mother or Father at a younger age. But I still feel alone at times. I feel sad and tired, at times. I dream about easier days when I am less exhausted.

Now that I am older and in my 40's myself, my life is still different from my friends. I have been helping my 87 year old Mama since my Papa passed away two years ago. She is so amazing; she lives on her own and still plays tennis. "Helping her," means just having fun with her; going to lunch, playing tennis, marketing, running errands, shopping and hanging out together. However, I am responsible and accountable for all of her life's "paperwork." This is the most challenging responsibility I have had so far. There is a weight on my shoulders to take good care of my Mama, like my Papa trusted I would do. It is not only the five year old that has to explain her Mama is not her Grandma to her friends, but it is the 40 year old that has to become the caregiver while her friends are still deciding which yoga class to take. Many people have lives harder than mine. My life is not unjustly hard. It is full of love and joy and I am one of the luckiest people on earth; partly because I had two of the most wonderful parents on earth. I am so glad I was born. I am so happy with my life. I am so lucky to have my Mama with me. We have so many happy times together and I love sharing life with her. My Mama makes me a better person, a less selfish person, a kinder person and a more patient person. She is my inspiration for love and selflessness. She always said her Mom was an angel, but I truly believe it is my Mama who is the angel. She is so loving and kind. She is happy and positive about everything in life. Even when life scares the hell out of her, she continues to stand up straight and tall and face the day with a smile. She never complains or pities herself. She is truly remarkable. If I can harness 40% of her energy and zest for life, it will be enough to carry me through.

Absence

My son is a tremendous athlete. Grandpa saw this as he was growing up. But what Grandpa didn't know was that he would continue to grow into an outstanding athlete in every sport he decided to play. The other day I was rereading a newspaper article written about my son being named to the All-CIF-Southern Section team for Division 1 in eight man football. He was the only freshman to be named to this All-State team, and unanimously at that. My son registered more than 100 tackles, returned two interceptions for touchdowns, and recovered five fumbles. On offense, he scored three touchdowns as well. Grandpa never got to see him play football.

His real love is baseball though. After my Papa died, my son had a game and knew I was in my score keeper position in the stands watching. He looked at me as he walked to be at bat. He looked up into the heavens and out into the outfield. He hit that ball clear over the fence and he and I knew it was for Grandpa.

And this, right this moment, is his first high school baseball season. I sit in the stands, watching him as he kneels behind home plate. He is an amazing catcher. He plays the position effortlessly, flawlessly and naturally. He is completely relaxed and thoroughly enjoying himself. He wants to be a professional baseball player and I already am picking out the RV Seth and I will buy when it's time to travel the country to watch his games. I believe in him and know whatever he sets out to accomplish, he will. He is extremely intelligent. He has tremendous strength and endurance, just like his Dad. He is focused and grounded and mature. He is also a very calm soul. This part of him reminds me of my Papa. I wish my Papa could be watching him grow up into the fine young man he is becoming. He was only 11 years old when my Papa passed away. He was still young, just starting to enter the pre-teen stage. He was big and strong but still had his baby chub. Shortly after my Papa died, my son grew straight up, thinned out and became stronger and bigger than most all the kids within a couple of years his age. My Mama always said my husband, Seth, was just like my Papa in so many ways. They both are extremely intelligent and unique men. Now, I see my son. He is so much like his own Dad, who is similar to my Papa. So I can only conclude that with my Papa's strength of character and my husband's strength of character and athletic abilities, my son has what it takes to make a great life for himself in whatever ways he chooses. I am just so sad my Papa will miss watching him grow up and that my Papa doesn't get to know my son as a young man. I am sad too that my son doesn't get to talk to his Grandpa and ask him questions about life. These are the things I think about as I sit in the stands watching my son perform so outstandingly.

Maypole Corollary

Before my Papa got sick, my husband and I were stable and effective. We were finally a two income household. We were beginning to save money and looked forward to a debt free, simple life style because our expenses were less than our income. Our children were in school and working was stress free because daylight hours were working hours and everyone had their job to do; the kids needed to get good grades and the parents needed to make money. It all made sense.

When my Papa got sick, I stopped working and for a while it was ok. But after a while, I couldn't make sense of what was expected of me. If I worked, someone was left out. The stress from not doing all my jobs well was overwhelming. If I didn't work, then everyone was cared for.

I am fully committed and loyal beyond doubt. I have not left my family behind, but I have left myself behind. How do I make what I need to do and what I want to do be one and the same? Well, I need to care for my family and I want to care for my family, so I am o.k. on that aspect. However, I am constantly thinking about others, so I need to learn to remember to think about myself.

I did try to start back to work in January, 2 years after my Papa died. But in July, I was reminded I was pushing myself to reenter the work force too quickly. I was, literally, writing out my first real estate purchase contract when my cell phone rang and the ladies my Mama played tennis with twice a week were on the other line. My Mama had fallen and hit her head. I grabbed my keys and ran to my truck. I raced to the high school tennis courts, while calling the local paramedics and ambulance service. When I arrived, my Mama was on the ground with the blazing sun shining on her. She was hot, confused and trying to get up.

111

"Mama, I'm here. I'm here Mama. It's o.k. I'll take care of you. The paramedics are coming to check you out and make sure you're ok."

"Oh, Rene, I am so sorry! I know you were selling a house today. I told the ladies not to call you and disturb you. I am so sorry! I am such a bother for you."

"Mama, you are not. I love you. I am so glad I am here with you. Now, don't worry about that right now. We need to focus on just making sure you are alright. Ok?"

"Ok. Rene, I am so glad you are here. I love you."

"I love you so much Mama!"

I followed behind the ambulance and it reminded me of another day I followed my Papa to the emergency room. It was his birthday and he was having trouble with his heart. As I stared at the ambulance in front of me, I felt very alone. I thought about my siblings and how they never have had to feel this responsibility. I thought about my children and how lucky I am they are healthy. I thought about my husband and how much I love him. I thought about my Papa. I thought about my poor, scared Mama and how I really wished I could be in the ambulance with her. Half way to the hospital, I thought about my client. I called my client and told him what had happened. I called my broker and told him what had happened. I called the other realtor and told him what had happened. And then I put them all together and said I am sorry but you will have to continue without me.

I lived at my Mama's house for three weeks. My daughter ran errands for us and my husband watched over our 14 year old son and his needs. I missed my family very much but I know I was lucky to be able to live with my Mama and take care of her. My husband has always been very understanding and good to me and my parents. He held down the fort while I was gone and understood how much my Mama needed me.

I haven't worked with clientele since. How can I commit to my career when I am needed by my family? My career was supposed to grow as my children grew older and needed me less. But now I find myself in this quandary where my career can't grow because I am the main caregiver at home; for all my family.

I call this life event the "Maypole Corollary."

My life seems to be a series of events that pull on me, while I stand firmly in one place. The people in my life dance around me while I hold the steady ground. I am the Maypole for the generation before and after me. I am the solid while they are the ribbon holders, encircling me. I am the caregiver, the moneymaker, the planner, the thinker, the responsible one, my husband and me, of course. We are the Maypole. The Maypole Corollary is the effect of my parents giving birth to me while in their 40's. In the future of our American society, we will see the

Maypole Corollary play out like never before in history. There is a 298% increase in parents having kids after 40 years old. How will it affect society, families, individuals, and the family economy?

Women and men, both, struggle to combine career and family. I have a career that has been many years in the making while I maneuvered around raising our children as our priority. As I said before, my career was supposed to grow as my children grew older and needed me less. When my Papa found out he had cancer, I let my broker know I would be taking time off. After my Papa passed, my broker let me go permanently; I hadn't come back to the workforce quick enough. My struggle to work is ongoing, so here is one of my concerns: (You may switch woman for man and daughter for son in any part of the coming sentence to be gender correct) the very woman who enjoys a career and then chooses to have children in her 40's is going to be the very reason her daughter may, one day, lose her job in order to take care of her elderly mother; ironic. This, of course, is only one very narrow perspective of one very specific scenario. Matter of fact, this scenario is not even the one I experienced. There are many reasons women and men choose to have children in their 40's and I don't want to simplify the situation. Many women and men try for many years to have children and it is not until they are in their 40's that they are able to get pregnant or find a surrogate mother or adopt a baby. Also, like my parents, some families just keep growing until the parents are in their 40's and still having children.

I would like to help someone avoid future difficulties by asking the questions, how will your adult child be affected by your age and how will you prepare for this time in your life? Your child may be affected emotionally, physically and financially by your older age. Your child's time commitments may be affected because of the time caring for an older parent, your child's emotional stability may be challenged with the responsibilities of elderly care, your child's financial capabilities may be hindered, and perhaps, your child's marriage may be strained because of the added emotional and financial stress. When a 20 year old has a child, their child is 60 years old and close to or is retired when helping with their elderly parent. When a parent is 40 and has a child, the child will most likely be in the nitty-gritty part of life; teenagers, career, far from retirement, car loans, home mortgage, etc., when helping with the elderly parent.

I believe many older parents are more financially stable and therefore will have an economic strategy in place. Economists, in early 2000, began equating a mother's contribution to the family economy in dollar amounts, i.e. child care while the father is working is worth $12 per hour times 40 hours per week equals $23,000 per year. In the same manner, a child's hours of attention toward his or her parent needs to be studied and evaluated in economic terms. According to a study by AARP, $450 billion dollars was the economic value of unpaid elderly care in the USA in 2009; a 21% increase over the study in 2007. 62 million Americans give uncompensated care; that is one in every four. I do believe we are moving toward more research in this area. What I see coming in the future is the impact on 40 year olds, as opposed to the impact on retired baby boomers today.

As I listen to radio stations and read reports, I am sympathetic to each person's experience. It makes me realize I need to talk with my Mama about our future sooner than later. There are such important topics we need to discuss, such as: would she ever consider living with us in our home? So far, she has stayed in the home where my Papa died. She found comfort in being in "their" home and maintaining her independence has priority.

The complexities lie in the fact that the future is unpredictable and yet, I need to prepare for it also. It's a very complex situation. As a matter of fact, raising questions in front of my Mama is difficult because it seems insensitive, but it's not; it is reality. And this reality makes me question how exactly this scenario should play out. I don't have the answer for myself, but I will try to create a solution. In hind sight, my Papa, Mama and I should have discussed five years and ten years into the future in more detail. It seemed like discussing three years into the future was preparation enough, but it wasn't. And of course at the time, my Papa was dying and we were barely strong enough to survive the present, let alone plan 10 years in advance. Now, my Mama and I must look into the future and decide what we want to do and this will be challenging because her areas of expertise were not planning, money management and emergency scenario preparedness.

I think it is important to realize and acknowledge this is not a one way street. My Mama has had her own challenges and difficulties. It must be difficult to allow her child to do things for her. I know she must have complicated feelings and thoughts about needing me; needing the child she once raised, to do and take care of her responsibilities. She must question how much she should rely on me, how many decisions she should make on her own and how many she should let me help her make. These questions and concerns will take my Mama and me to a place of discussion that is unfamiliar to us, but while it is about her future, it is also about my future; it is about our future and it is the "our" that we are still coming to understand. To acknowledge and evaluate this future is of the utmost importance.

Silver Lining

The silver lining to my father passing is my relationship with my Mama has grown and deepened beyond what I ever expected. I have learned from watching my Mama that a person growing older is still growing. Psychological development is an ongoing, dynamic process. She still questions who she is and what gives her life meaning, just as a younger person would. I have heard elderly people countless times say while they know they are 80 years old, in their hearts and mind's eye, they are still young. Our culture is brutal to the elderly; I have experienced this now first hand. My hope is our society will start to examine the body of knowledge related to successful aging. As I learned in my anthropology classes in college, "It is not the strongest of the species that survives, nor the most intelligent, but the one most responsive to change." Charles Darwin's research on adaptation as the criterion for determining success for any organism needs to be applied to the aging process.

We need to discuss and teach what it means to successfully change and adapt in our older years and to our aging needs. Our society cannot afford to wait until each individual becomes old or takes care of someone old, to think about what it means to be old. Changes in our life cycle are discussed in depth when it comes to childhood development; i.e. Your Two Year Old: Terrible or Tender, by Louise Ames. Yet, everyone shies away from talking about what it means to grow old and how to successfully grow old. Can you imagine a book, Your 74 Year Old: Grumpy or Senile? I experience this avoidance when talking to my friends and it is one of the reasons taking care of my Mama has been so isolating for me. When I start to talk about what responsibilities I have, or what my commitments entail, my friends' eyes glaze over. I can tell they would rather talk about anything other than what the day consists of for an old person. The idea the old are the closest to death is a falsehood, but a fabrication none the less that frightens people away from talking about or to older people. Each and every one of us does not know when our time will come to leave this world. In 1900 the life expectancy in the USA was 48.3 years old for females. It may be a romantic notion the elderly in times gone by were respected as wise, but then again, the elderly were only in their 40's. We need a paradigm shift in our thinking about what it means to grow old. I call it the "Elderly Myth" and this cultural myth needs to be examined. Discussions in the universities should take place and young adults should think about what it means to them to successfully age throughout their entire life span. My Mama was playing tennis twice a week when she was 87 years old; I choose to envision my elderly years on the road, surfing with my husband and traveling the planet. I challenge everyone, how do you envision yourself at 87 years old?

The most important daily decision for my Mama and what keeps her going is to have an interest in the day. Her calendar of events is her cornerstone. The trick is to not be so busy she gets worn down, but to be busy enough that life is exciting. She has always played tennis twice to three times a week and when she had to give it up, we needed to find something else for her to do. She now goes to the gym and takes a class twice a week; Silver Sneakers has been a god send for her. Being social is crucial. I try to have something planned for several times a week where my Mama and I can spend the day busy. We have marketing, shopping, luncheons and doctor appointments to attend. Our Friday lunch is very important and we never miss it. Recently, with my daughter getting married, we have had a lot of fun with the planning and preparations of the wedding. Life has more meaning when it is shared across generations.

When I began my book, I never could have anticipated my writing would inspire my Mama and, in turn, she would inspire me. She sought out some of her writings she wrote when she was "83 years young" about her childhood and she shared them with me.

What a transformational experience for me! I got to read about the distant past, a life time so different from today and so different from my own, yet it is me and it is my own. It's an ancestral timeline, cross-generational experiences coming together to bond lives and hearts.

When I was studying to be an anthropologist, I learned that individual life stories are one method of gathering information to understand a group of people, whether a large community, a village or a small tribe. I would like to present to you the life story of the women in my own family. To think you will know almost as much about my past as I do is quite interesting to me and makes me wonder how much do we really know about ourselves. I know my Mama well, but I don't know her Mother. These stories are my treasure. These stories lend an understanding of who I am. As I reread what I wrote about my Mama's Mother earlier on in this book, it occurs to me I have known her all along. My stories match what my Mama talks about, yet I only knew a tidbit. We are raised with stories and experiences that sculpt us into who we are, whether we know and understand it or not. Sometimes who we think we are on the surface is the same person we are so down deep. That is why we are able to pull through in difficult times, because when we reach deep down inside ourselves we actually have more of ourselves than we could ever imagine. We have generations of strength inside, ancestral code runs through our veins and that genetic code is a part of who we are; countless relatives building upon experiences and gathering emotions and abilities that are encoded into us and available to us to rely on and use if we choose.

I'm honored to share my Mama's childhood with you; a window with a view into our past:

The Apron Years

"They tell me my father was a handsome man when he was younger. He had lots of black curly hair as a boy and kept his grey hair until he was hit by a hit-and-run car and died. My Mother met and married Dad while he was in uniform (WWI) and took care of Dad's Mother during their marriage. Grandma was quite a handful and bedridden most of the time.

As a very young child, even before Kindergarten I have just pieces of a jig-saw puzzle of my life I remember. But certain things stand out more than others. When I was around 4 years old, in Kansas, my Great Grandmother died and my Mother sat by her bed. In those days when someone died, they laid the person on the bed and someone sat with them until burial. All the children played outside while the women were making food. My sister and I were dressed so pretty with our new bonnet Mom had made. My sister dropped hers in the 2-holer (that in those days was the outhouse or toilet.) We were digging for it with a big stick, when Mom found out. We got a good spanking.

I remember prekindergarten, playing under the kitchen table and running out just as my Mother carried a big pot of soup to the table. I was burnt down my back and although I don't remember the pain I am still remembering the sobbing until I fell asleep. Whatever my Mom did for me, I have no scars.

I remember during this time period visiting Grandma on the chicken farm and being able to climb up on her big feather bed to sleep. It probably wasn't as soft and tall as I remembered, but it was so wonderful and warm. I can still see my Grandma in later years churning butter and separating the milk and making dill pickles and sauerkraut in the big stone crock. They always had wells outside their kitchen where they lowered the milk and butter to keep cold. Also dirt cellars where they stored food and all the jars and jars of her canning of food. (They could also go to the cellar in case of cyclones.)

They always had a hand pump in the kitchen for water and never had a bathroom until 1960. I remember my Grandparents as such hard workers. It was horses and hay wagons, windmills, milking cows, etc. When they lived on the big farm they had certain time for the butchering of cows and pigs. All neighbors helped and divided the meat. It was a horrible sight for a young kid to watch. After Grandpa grew too old to tend a farm, they moved across the street from the high school and he was the custodian of the school. He would be up at dawn to shovel snow and get the furnaces to heat the school, clean all rooms, wax the gym floor and wax the school desks.

I don't remember my parents fighting during my pre-kindergarten, but my Mother, brother, sister and I moved in with my Grandparents for a short time in the big Stone farm house. My brother had to bring in the cows every night, but I just played tea-party with Virginia a lot. I must have been stung by bees at least every week, because I sure remember all the bees, hornets, and snakes at that place. Grandpa would put me on top of the old horse and give me rides. Grandpa was very religious. He was the pastor of his church and we never ate without prayers and church every Sunday (sometimes twice on Sunday). But he was so nice and everyone knew and loved him. Except they were very hard on my Mother when she was growing up, which they finally asked my Mother for forgiveness before they died and she of course did. Grandpa thought most T.V. was sinful. So, we didn't dare turn on T.V. while they visited because the girls were showing too much leg! He is probably turning in his grave with all the T.V. today. My Grandma never cut her hair, but always in a bun. When we were living in the big stone farm house, I guess my Mom and Dad got together again and we moved to the City. Children never knew the grown-up world. If they were having hard times we never knew about it. In those days, the men or fathers never showed a lot of affection to children. They left child rearing to women. My Mother more than made up for it. No matter she was so tired she could drop or so busy, she'd always have time for us. She was our disciplinarian and gave us so much love. I loved her so much, that I still miss her and think about her always.

When we moved I was not old enough for school. I remember watching all the kids play because our house was across from the play area. I remember no bathtub and Mom filled a huge galvanized tub in the kitchen. Brother always got first bath, then Virginia and me. But we did have a toilet! When I say my Mother was the disciplinarian I mean she told Virginia and me not to go out of our yard boundary and she told us exactly which crack not to cross on the sidewalk. When we thought she wasn't looking we just went a little ways over the crack. My Mother never took a hand to us, but she always had a little switch (off a tree) handy. Our little legs had welts on them! We knew Mom meant what she said, but she did it with love in mind.

My father had many jobs. First he worked at the Flour Mill and when that shut down he was a carpenter. With Depression upon us and hard times, they both worked the Chicken Plucking Bldg. Not for long. Dad also was Deputy

Sheriff for some time. Then Mom started washing and ironing for Doctors and nurses at the Hospital. That way she could be home with us kids. Then Dad started pick-up and deliveries and keeping the books. Then Mom was so good that all the wealthy people on the hill wanted her. Dad hung all the wash on clotheslines outside. But Mom was washing more than 14-15 washes on Monday and around 10 on Thursday. On Tuesday and Wednesday and Friday she ironed. The day was usually 5:00 am till 6:00 pm in bed by 9:00. She bartered everything. Remember we were in depression but we never knew it because we had a Doctor that did everything we needed, we had milk, eggs and butter, food, ice cream. She just bartered with anything we needed. All the time Virginia was layed up with scarlet fever and nearly died; the Dr. visited every day and food came to us every day. Brother and I had to play outside with snow up to our knees. Eat lots of oranges and fruit. Get warm by the big pot belly stove right next to Virginia and to bed early. God watched over us because I never even got the sniffles.

One time in the middle of the night the ambulance came for my Mother. We didn't know she was hurting but she had a hernia and her guts were coming out. She nearly died but Virginia and I were at our bedroom window upstairs on our knees and praying and crying so hard. Afterwards the Dr. told her to take it easy, but that wasn't my Mother's nature and later on she nearly paid for her life again when it occurred again. Like I said my Mother did the hard work, my father picked up and delivered and kept the books, oh yes, and hung clothes. While my Mother was ironing clothes I could sit by the hour and have her repeat all the old songs and verses she had learned. She had a great knack at writing poems and remembering all the songs and verses. I still have some she did. I'll never forget one Christmas my sister and I got our first "big" baby dolls. By the time my Mother could afford them, we were almost too old for them. That same Xmas I got my Doll, the Dr. said I narrowly averted death. It was cold winter time, but Virginia and I wanted to show off our Dolls, but I felt so sick we hardly made it out the door and I had to go back. Mom put us upstairs to bed and blamed it all on Xmas candy. The fumes of a gas water heater which had no odor, had poured through the house. First it was Virginia and I in bed, then Brother and then Mother. Dad had been going outside all the time to hang clothes on the line. I tried to make the bathroom and fell several times. Dad just happened to come inside when he thought he heard a fall. When he found me unconscious he called the Dr. The first thing the Dr. did seeing all of us in bed was open every window and door to let the bitter cold in. He stuck my whole body out the window to survive me and said I was nearly dead. (Well, I made the papers!) The youngest is the first to go, and then Virginia and then Brother, etc.

As a little girl (up to 5th or 6th grade) I always wanted to be a dancer or actress. I guess that is why I played paper dolls so much. I would make all the clothes for my paper doll and sit by the hour playing with Patty across the street. She lived upstairs in an apt. house and we played on the steps so we wouldn't bother anyone. Then I played cars with "Veryl Dean Swarty." Veryl Dean always had a lot of cars and toys. We put a curtain up in his basement of the apt. bldg with the help of the janitor. We charged everyone a penny to watch our play and song and dance that we made up as we went. I'm sure they all thought it was a waste of a penny.

When summer was on us it was so-o hot that everyone (kids) would get to put their mattresses out in the back yard and sleep outside. It was still at this home when every Sat night Virginia and I would go to the show and Mom and Dad parked in front of 5 & 10 cent store called "Duckwalls." Brother worked there and we'd wait until he got off work and then Dad would come get Virginia and me from the movie and we'd go home. Mom loved gossiping with everyone coming into town on Sat night. We usually had crackers and bologna when we got home.

Mom always baked her own bread and rolls, pies, etc. I don't know too much about it, but she had what they call a "starter" to start more bread. I was always a bit embarrassed when I took out my lunch at school and I always had home-made bread for sandwiches, while the others had nice soft bread. But everyone could smell the bread baking for houses around. Mom always made cinnamon rolls too and any left-over dough she put some cinnamon on (with sugar) and passed out to all of us kids waiting to get some.

We never realized that Mom was probably making more money during depression than anyone in town. The wealthy people still had money during depression. My Mother finally divorced my Dad after we were older. I was 6th or 7th grade. My Dad was raised with little affection he had never hugged or kissed us as children like Mother. It was a shock to us because they never argued and my Dad told us one Sat night sitting at the kitchen table, crying like a baby. After they were divorced, my Aunt and Uncle (with their children) were so desperate and could not meet their rent payments, so they moved in with us and took over helping Mom. The very unfair part was they took 1/3-1/3-1/3. (Mom-Aunt-Uncle) But they were like that, and Mom needed help to keep going. Course Mom had 3 children and they had two. But Mom never complained. After about a year my Mother started losing a lot of weight. She had always been heavy, but little did we know that she has a reason to look trim. Her very dear friend asked her to visit on Sunday. The children stayed home. There she met Frank who was divorced and came from California.

Now Frank was Mom's first and only true love since grade school. My grandfather forbade them to be together because he thought Frank was a sinner. He smoked and didn't go to church and a real wild guy for those days, probably not bad according to now days. His father was a Dr. Anyway they always sneaked out to see each other and be together. They couldn't get married so with WWI Frank enlisted at 17 and went over to France. He fought a terrible war in the trenches. They used mustard Gas on the men and Frank had red burns on his legs. They would feed them liquor before going over the trench and I do believe with that, and Navy Life later on, he became an alcoholic. Well, he was reported dead and my mother then met my Father. I am sure she never quite got over her true love. But later in life to meet again!!! (My Mother was always "old" to me and she was probably all of 36-38 years old. She always said "She felt old as a child even.") Little did we know that my Mother was dating someone, but she did seem happy. She asked us if we'd like to move to California. All we could think of was "Hollywood" and "ocean". She gave the business over to my Aunt, sold everything that wouldn't fit in a small trailer and off to California. Brother drove (He was 18 - Virginia16 -me 14). We arrived in L.A. and stayed at a friend's apt. with her and her son. We were told nothing, and had no idea, but there was Frank waiting too. Mom and Frank ran off and got married and he bought the smallest house I'd ever seen out in the country called, "Lynwood." He started building a bedroom, bathroom, a kitchen eating area and back porch. Needless to say, we three kids weren't that happy. I started the ninth grade which in Jr. High is

7,8,9,10 in Lynwood and then the 11,12th and Jr. college in Compton. My sister and Brother went thru Jr. College, but the World War II came along in my 12th grade and I never made the Jr. College.

In my 11th year I met Audrey Halverson and we became best friends. I was dancing at the "Paladium" and "Trianon" to the very best bands. Duke Ellington, Tommy Dorsey, Jimmy Dorsey, Glenn Miller, and the list goes on. That was when Frank Sinatra was just a singer with the band. I know this one boy that always danced in Movie Pictures as x-tras. So in 1940-41? Sept 2nd I went to Columbia Studios Set #7 and we did a jitterbug scene that I never saw, but one night my folks watching a movie they saw me. After the war started we used to go to what was called the "Swing Shift dances" because of everyone working swing shifts which were 12 midnight till 2 or 3 am. Mom worried about me, but Pop would tell her that dancing kept me happy and out of trouble.

War came out in Dec. 1941 and the soldiers started moving on to our campus grounds in 1942. But during my 12th yr. a group of us girls had a club called "Alpha Amazons" and we had a good sum of money and decided to send our money into Hollywood to entertain troops. They called us up and asked if we would like to go with some entertainment. It was so much fun. We took a bus with them. We went to the Hospital with Nat King Cole and talked to the soldiers that couldn't leave their beds. We went to Palm Springs and put up in the beautiful Hotel. (I think I still have the letter thanking us) We went with "Spike Jones" and with one of the

Dorsey Bro. In Palm Springs they were all sitting on the grass and the band on the stage, and we would talk with the boys. That was Sept. 19, 1942. Audrey and I also joined "Ambulance Core" that once every month would travel by Army Trucks to an army base and hold a dance. We had to sign a paper that we would not give our addresses away and we would always be on the truck when we would go home. It was always in the evening and very well chaperoned.

After I graduated, Pop wanted back in the Navy to fight the war. He was probably around 45. Mom and him had to move to Alameda Air Base near San Francisco. So Audrey and I decided we'd live in our house and we both worked at Sears Roebuck in L.A

I and Audrey made a couple of trips on "Troop Trains" to visit Mom and Pop.

No one had cars to drive during the war, so the train was the only way to travel from Lynwood to San Francisco. All the trains were always full of soldiers moving from place to place. I met a soldier on one trip that I wrote to all during the war. I remember one trip when Mom met us and she was a bruise from her eyes to the bottom of her neck. I felt like crying! She had just had every tooth in her head pulled at once. They said it was poison in her gums. Which I'm sure they could help her now days to save her teeth. She had all of her teeth. I begin to get homesick to be with her (Mom) and they (Mom, Pop and Virginia) couldn't get a place to live without me coming and getting a job at the Naval Air Station. All the officers and enlisted men's quarters were full, but they had some housing for people who worked on the "Base." So Audrey moved back to her home (several blocks away) and Mom rented out our house and I moved to Alameda. I applied for a job on the Air Base and to my surprise got a job as file clerk in the administrative bldg in Administrative office. That enabled us to move right in to a 3 bedroom housing right next to the Base. So Virginia, Mom and Pop and I lived there. Pop was a "chief" in the Navy and worked in the Aviation Repair on the Base, but came home every evening. My Aunt and Uncle left Kansas and came out to Alameda Ca. to work in the shipyard on the Base. Their daughter was married to a Flier who was shipped overseas and she lived with her Mom and Dad and her other sister lived with them. They both worked on the Base as secretaries. They all lived in the next housing to us, so Mom had her sister and Virginia to talk to. My brother finally joined the Navy and stationed at Mare Island so his wife and Baby lived with us too. Virginia gave birth while living there. The letter came that "Mac" (Virginia's husband) was missing in action. We didn't let her know until after the birth of their baby, since the letter came right before she was going to have the baby. Everyone thought she was taking it so well, but I shared a bedroom with her and heard her crying every night. It was a very sad time for her.

Well the war was over in 1945, so Mom, Pop, Virginia, the baby, Brother and his family were all going back to Lynwood, Ca. I was having so much fun dating from Lt. Cdr of a ship to the lowly sailor in Communications that I wasn't ready to give it all up and move back to Lynwood. So I moved in with my Aunt and Uncle and their daughter and husband (in the navy). I paid 1/3 of all food and I slept in the back porch on a bed. Eventually when my Mother visited me, she was so disturbed with the set-up that she wanted me home. Well I was 21 ½ years old and time to move on.

But during the time I lived with my Aunt the "Base" decided to put on a stage show, "Fiddlers Green." They had me featured in "Home State Side" song and we danced several dances. I had to learn some tapping, etc and I was doing something I only dreamed of. I hate to say it, but the war time was very exciting for me since I was 18 thru 22 during this time.

So I moved to Lynwood Ca. and lived with Mom and Pop. I was hoping to take a vacation from work, but Audrey (my girlfriend) said "there's an opening at my work, please interview for a job." I was hired! I was anxious to put on some dancing shoes so Audrey and I started going to the "20-30" dance, 1946-1947, which was held every Thursday night in Compton. It was like a "Youth Center" of today. So many of the kids I went to school with were meeting again.

One night Carl came in, (without his uniform on) and he says "I saw you across the room and decided you're the one." We danced together all night and I let him take me home. He told me he was still in the Navy and we made a date for the following Sat. He happened to have duty on board the ship as Officer in Charge that Saturday. He sent the "Capt's Gig" to pick me up and bring me to the ship. We had dinner served to us and I still laugh to myself when I think of all the ambiance and then we are served meatloaf! Then I was given the choice of any movie I wanted to see, of course whatever I picked, the enlisted men had to watch too. I don't even remember what I picked or saw because most of the time Carl and I were watching the stars. It was so romantic! You have heard _An Officer and a Gentleman_. Well that was my Carl. That was the beginning of our life. Carl got out of the Navy shortly after our dating and decided to go back to college and he graduated in June 1948 with Bachelor of Science. But during his time at college we dated all the time. I was also serenaded by the Fraternity Bros of Carl's and Pinned by Carl and it is like an engagement. Carl and I both remember the movie and time that he actually proposed to me. We had just seen _Captain from Castile_ with Tyrone Power and then went up on the crest of the hills above Hollywood and he proposed! We both took marriage very seriously, but we were in love, and felt we could spend the rest of our life with that person. We had been going out with each other for 2 years and it was time.

I took all my lessons to become a Catholic so our marriage would not have any conflict. We had a big church wedding with Gown etc and honeymooned at Palm Springs. We both worked so we didn't have a long honeymoon. We rented an apt. in Maywood close to my work and Carl worked in Brea. When I was 6 ½ mo. pregnant I quit work and Carl and I moved in with my Sister Virginia and her son until I had our first child. We then bought our first home. We were only in a short while when Carl had to leave for the Korean War. It was hard for both of us and many loved filled letters. With WWII I was dating and having fun, but now I was without my love, Carl, who was fighting a war. He came back to the States and before he was mustard out I became pregnant with our second girl. We decided for a bigger home so bought 3 bedroom 2 bath home. 8 years later we had our boy so we decided to move again. This time 5 bedroom, 4 baths. And again 8 years later we had a girl Rene. So I didn't want to move again."

"When I think of my Mother I always see her with her apron on. She put it on over her housedress in the morning and didn't remove it until she cleaned up after supper was over. It was usually a very big apron that encircled her and tied in the back. It always had pockets for the many handkerchiefs for wiping her brow or to give to us children when we hurt ourselves and the tears would come. Maybe that apron with its many pockets was a sign of protection when she folded it around us if we were cold or hurt. The smell of the apron was whether she was baking pies or bread or just the smell of the laundry she worked so hard on, but it was a part of my Mother. She comforted us and made us feel safe and secure. There was always a pocket with a hanky to wipe our nose on. I find myself always carrying a hanky for my children if they need it. I guess it symbolizes the love of a Mother to her children. The apron is just one of the many things I remember about my Mother. She's in heaven now, probably making beautiful aprons for the angels."

"My Dear Mother

When did I notice my Mother's hands

Grow knarled and pricked with blood,

While sewing on quilts and hand me downs,

When there was no one there to judge.

Did I see her eye-sight going? When she couldn't see at all?

When she felt her way around the room,

so we wouldn't see her fall!

Why didn't I tell her I loved her so—

and please to not grow old!

It's 3 little words, Mothers love to hear

and they're words that should be told,

We let the many years go by, and

Still we seem to wait,

Then "of a sudden" you see the lines, and then

its' all too late

Oh! Mother Dear how much you were loved,

and how much you now are missed!

The last "parting" on this earth, was your

cold cheek which I kissed.

I miss and love you, Mother Dear, and

wish that I could be,

As loved by all my children, as you

were loved by me!"

These are the words I will be left holding one day when I can no longer hold my Mama. I don't have any of my Papa's words to hold and read. I don't know what his young life was like except for the stories he told me. I try to hold on to the words in my head but I am sure one day I will not remember one event and the next year I will forget another. That is how life tends to be; slowly we create memories and slowly we forget them.

Surfing and Getting Back To My Roots

I went surfing for only the second time since my Papa got sick, almost four years ago. The water felt refreshing. There is no "feeling your age" in the water. As soon as I started to paddle out into the surf, time was irrelevant and I felt like I have felt my entire life in the surf, young, vibrant and exhilarated. Surfing is healing. Surfing is meditative. Surfing is a gift in my life from my husband to me; a gift I will always cherish.

If I could capture the feeling in a bottle, I would be rich. The sun was warm, the air was cool, a slight breeze blew in from the Pacific Ocean. The ocean was calm and the waves were perfect for me. There was a nice paddling channel along the southern rock outcropping, there was a sweet little southern swell and the waves lined up with the Sea Chest Restaurant and the outside reef; peeling waves that went both right and left. I was smiles the entire afternoon. Wave after wave, I felt so relieved and free of worry. After I surfed, I fell asleep on the beach next to the cliff. I was so relaxed. I can't remember how many decades it has been since I fell asleep on the beach, perhaps since college!

Today, I am a bit sore in my chest from paddling and I have a million things to do, but they are good things and I look forward to my day. My daughter is getting married! I have five months to plan a wedding. We are all so excited. I am beyond happy for the two little love birds. Young love, aaahhhh. I also have my son's baseball game to go to, in a city that is an hour and a half away. But first, I have to take a shower, pick my Mama up from the hair salon and go to lunch with her. Afterwards, I have to do some laundry, clean the morning dishes from breakfast for the boys, water the greenhouses, weed the front yard before my neighbors are disappointed, feed the pets, pay some bills, deal with our student loans being sold to another company, follow up on a real estate lead, tidy up the house, call my Mama's insurance company and make sure her vehicle is correctly insured and confirm the caterer for Kai's wedding; just another day in the life of a busy American.

Relax

Ah, it feels good. Relax, Rene. Everything is ok. Everyone is fine. It's alright to take some time for yourself. You don't have to rush to clean your son's baseball uniform; he can wear it dirty one time in his life. The wedding wine does not have to be bought today in Paso Robles. The floors can be a little dirty and the kitchen can look like you cooked in it today. Life is going by so quickly. Slow down and don't worry. You are not a gourmet cook; don't fret that your family's dinner is once again chicken and broccoli. You are not Wonder Woman, but you are a good person. You are doing your best and you are a good Mama. You are not perfect, but you are a good wife. You are not with your Mama every day, but you are a good daughter. Relax. Enjoy life.

I knew I had to take time for myself. I just didn't know how or what I should be doing. Running was not appealing and all that my mind wanted to do was think. So when I was in the shower one morning, I wrote on the steamy shower door with my finger,

"Dear 40 Year Old Parent & Miracle Child."

It was such a simple sentence; it was such an enormous idea. In my mind's eye, I had been a writer my entire life. My earliest image of who I thought I would become was created when I was a very, very young child; it was an image of a young woman gathering water from a stream and living in a forest. This woman was a writer and the forest was her magical place where her imagination was free. I later became an Anthropologist with a similar image in mind; to leave a society in which rules are written in stone and to explore an intellectual world where cultural differences are explored, accepted and respected. I wrote letters, poems, songs, and junk my entire life; most of it junk. My best poem I rendered into my husband's cell phone as a message, then threw the written page into the fire as an offering to the gods for having inspired such greatness. I can hear bits and pieces in my brain once in a while but never again will I hear its beauty.

When I decided to write this book, it was as though I came down with a virus. I hid my doings for many months, not wanting to share with anyone I had started writing a book. I finally told my husband what I was doing because I was worried sick he would begin to think I was having an internet affair because of all the hours I was spending on the computer. I was also waking up in the middle of the night, in a cold sweat, with a powerful need to write. So I told him what my intentions were and, with that, became more comfortable sitting at my desk for long periods of time. My goal was 17,000 words; roughly the amount of words of my favorite author, John Steinbeck, and his short novel, <u>The Pearl</u>. You know; the thin book you grab in high school when your book report is due the next day. My second goal was 27,000 words; roughly the amount of words in, <u>The Old Man and The Sea</u>, by Ernest Hemingway. I knew I was not capable of writing, <u>East of Eden</u>, my favorite book of all time, but if other normal, simple, average people could write memoirs, then why couldn't I? Of course, my life was not as exciting and extraordinary as Jeanette Walls' life, portrayed brilliantly in <u>The Glass Castle</u>, my drop dead favorite memoir, but I believe in all people being given a voice. The simple question being; what makes you unique? I have told you what made me unique growing up and still to this day. I am the only 43 year old, whom I know, who can recall the Great Depression with second hand accounts of what is was like to live through the famous time period.

When I hit my 17,000 word goal, I told my Mama I was writing a book. I didn't tell her what it was about, I only told her the title. She liked what I said about being unique. She realized she herself is a unique individual with fond childhood memories. Many of these childhood memories had been stored away in her mind and heart. My Papa was more talkative and tended to have center stage when it came to storytelling and childhood memories. My Mama didn't speak a lot about herself; she simply and silently and without complaint, took care of our needs.

After we spoke about my endeavor, she began to write again. My Mama, almost 89 years old, is writing! She is inspired. She is enjoying a process that is available to everyone, but few take advantage of it for some reason. Perhaps, we don't think we are important enough to put down in words our life story. I know I have struggled with this idea throughout the editing process. Writing the book, in the beginning, was fun. But when I had to finish it and conclude it was something worthwhile to pursue and publish, I questioned whether it was worthy. Was my life worthy of recall? Well, when I read what my Mama had written of her life story, I told her how honored I was to read her words. She is an amazing person and a beautiful writer. Once again, she shared with me something she wrote as an older woman of 66 years. I read her words about an age I will not reach for another 23 years. 66 years old; a time in my life that seems so far away. Am I prepared for my 60's? What expectations do I have of myself at that age? What cultural myths is my mind playing for me to pick from? Will I be a surfer traveling with my husband, a doting grandmother, a real estate agent? I once read a plaque on a man's desk that read,

"No man plans to fail, he only fails to plan."

Will I have planned for my retirement correctly? Will I even be retired? I reread my Mama's words. They echo her thoughts of a younger woman. My parents planned well and their life was comfortable. Yet, my Mama's words tell of the discomfort in a life in which society had not discussed what was valued and expected of an older woman moving across stages; changing from mother to retired housewife:

Great Expectations

"By now my children have gone away to school, have marriages, or just living on their own. By this time I've reached past middle age and I have ceased to struggle for my place in the world. I cannot go back to the tightly closed world of Romantic love and children. I have grown too old for a new career and raising new families. The American people, with our terrific emphasis on youth- action- and material success have belittled the woman of 60's. It is ridiculous to think I can look like I did in my 20-30's, but why am I made to feel that I should? Middle age is not a period of decline and approaching death, it should be a restful time of thinking "a job well done." It is hard to see ourselves as others see us, our hearts are young but our bodies seem to say differently. Some people try to escape into depression, love affairs or health problems. That is why my family is so important. Actually they will be my cane to lean on in my needs. God gave us a sacrament of marriage, but he didn't make it easy or perfect. It is one of the greatest gifts to be able to withstand all problems and meeting them face on. Marriage can form many bonds and in those bonds are many kinds of love. It is hard to imagine that two people, so different, can live together for years, without straining those bonds almost to a breaking point. You start out with such a romantic love that if there are any faults, you don't care or even want to think about them. Then the slow-growing love that you hardly know you have. It is companionship and mostly a sharing of every experience. It is a web of memories of conflicts, triumphs and disappointments. It is communication or lack of communication, likes and dislikes, agreeing or disagreeing, reactions to each other's habits. Marriage is just day to day living.

When you love someone, you do not love them all the time, in exactly the same way from minute to minute. Marriage is like a dance. We are both confident of the steps we take and do not have to change our rhythm to the other persons, we are perfectly in time. Of course I'll have to inject, that sometimes the floor is too sticky, the music too fast or too slow, but like all marriages, it takes a lot of give and take.

As I look at my daughters, my nieces, etc. they are better Mothers, admitted equals of men in intelligence and initiative. They are more courageous, more confident of what they want to do and more efficient in carrying through their aims. They are definitely more aware. But I wonder if they are causing more burden on themselves than they can bear. The bearing of children, rearing, feeding and educating them and running of a house, cleaning, cooking, relationship of spouse, pulls in every direction, and to be called freer with more opportunities is now questionable. We (such as myself) never see results of our work as a man does his work (such as "made more money," "have better job," "prestige" or someone admiring what they have accomplished, new home, new car, etc) How does one point to house hold chores and say "oh how clean the wash is", "the stools look clean," or the many errands thru life of Dr. appts, marketing, cooking, sewing and say "what a great job." With any free time from house we throw ourselves into committees and causes just to hear praise of some kind. In olden times the spot-less home was not the upper most importance. Now it is expected of us to have a spotless home, entertain, and be Mrs. U.S.A."

In the 1970's, what I call the Wonder Woman Syndrome in which a woman was expected to perform all of her traditional roles plus hold down a lucrative career, plus look like Wonder Woman, belittled my mom's traditional role of being a "housewife". That is why I went to graduate school. That is why I have a career. We, as a society, change and the successful people adapt to these changes. Darwin would say we are surviving. How did my Mama survive? She adapted. Her life changed from the stage of being a full time Mama, to my Papa's traveling companion to a widowed Elder. She adapted to these changes and it is why she is living today. But when she was 66 years old, expectations of her were confusing; her children were out of the house so she didn't spend as many hours cooking, cleaning and taking care of family members. Many women had gone back to work in their late 40's after their children were grown, but my Mama had me at that age. She was raising me from the time she was 45 until 63 years old. At 66 years old, she had just retired from motherhood. Was she all of a sudden supposed to jump into the work force after 40 years of being a "housewife"? That would have been very difficult. So what was her new role? Was my Mother still responsible for feeding my Papa, cleaning his clothes, cleaning the house by herself? Her friends no longer did the household chores because when they went back to work they started hiring people to clean for them and started eating out more. My Mama recounts many of her friends telling her how they refused to cook for their husbands. Why should they? They worked too! It was a time of transition, yet there weren't really any cultural expectations of what the new roles were for someone like my Mama. My Papa sold his company and retired from the workforce when I left for college. My parents had the day to do with as they pleased. Some people take care of grandchildren. Some people busy themselves around the house. My parents started traveling the world. My parents lived through a paradigm shift; people were living longer, were healthier into older years and their roles were being remodeled. My Papa never imagined he would be able to do so much after the age of 62. When he was a young man, men at 62 were sedentary. Traveling the world was his goal and he achieved it. It wasn't really what my Mama wanted to do, but it was my Papa's lifelong dream. So, my Mama traveled. She is glad she did and she now recounts her fond memories of traveling with my Papa in amazement she did so much.

Parents today, having children while in their 40's, are winging it; they, like my parents, have no social guidelines or examples to follow. They will have to restructure what their roles are in life. Have we as a society discussed this new role of a Mom and Dad in their 50's and 60's? Once again, social dynamics are changing and people are adapting. What seems odd today will be normal in the next decade. I question though, not only what will be the parents' experience, but also, what will the children experience?

When my Papa died, I was left asking, what is my role today? I understood my life stages as they related to my husband and children. But when my Papa died, what was expected of me and how was I supposed to adapt successfully? The Maypole Corollary is the most recent paradigm shift. People, once again, are living to be much older and on top of that, people are choosing to have children at 40 years old. What do we expect of older parents and what do they expect of themselves? Do parents of a 15 year old retire when they turn 62? Do children take care of their elderly parents when they are in their 40's and still taking care of their own children? These questions may seem silly to a farmer who never retires or to a family who already lives with three generations in the home, but for the modern couple, these questions asked early on, will make adapting to life stages a little bit easier.

Hope

There is a yearning and a wanting in my chest that pulls on me late at night. I reach my arm upward, my hand grasping for the heavens, hoping to discover a feeling or a helping hand perhaps. I have always felt this desire for more. But last night I wondered if I am simply a fool. Perhaps there is no more than this for me. Perhaps I have been too proud of myself for too little. But something inside of me tells me that if I give in, if I let down my guard and start to believe I am nothing special at all, then what I will be left with is anxiety and stress. I have to keep believing in myself. I can't sink down into hopelessness and helplessness. We are all human, earth-bound and meager, but something inside all of us wants to reach for the stars.

Writers are able to show the human condition through their stories. I fall so short of talent and skill I question whether I am worthy of telling my story. What I do know though is this; what I have told you is the truth; it is my life, my very simple life, and it is also my pain and my struggle to adapt. I hope whatever tomorrow brings I will be strong enough to meet the challenge, to adapt to the changes in my life and, I hope with all my heart, no matter how much pain I feel, I will always feel life is special.

Chapter 6

Fifth Life Stage: Wisdom

"Good night. Sweet dreams."

My 40+ year old parents taught me to cherish the people in my life: each and every person, the fun and the difficult, the grumpy and the nice, the helpful ones and the ones that need my help. The lives we have been blessed with living are the true gift of life and the love we are able to experience is the most valuable possession in this world. Life will always be difficult and there are always more turbulent times ahead, so hold the person next to you, forgive them of their faults and the ways they may have hurt you because they are who you will need one day. Treat them well and they will be there for you when you are the one in need. Don't take for granted your health, your beauty, your smile or your happiness. Strive to grow and become a better person, but never forget to appreciate what has been given to you.

I will always appreciate the life my parents gave to me in their older tender age of their fifth decade. They gave to me life and filled that life with love. They are my heroes and my inspiration for goodness.

I want all of you children, born to the wave of older parents who have become so abundant in the new millennium, to believe you are a miracle, appreciate the life that has been gifted to you and thank your parents for wanting to have you.

Even though my Papa didn't get to say "Happy 50th Birthday, Love", I felt that loving thought every day of my life; "Happy day, Love." No one knows how life will turn out. The best we can do is to do our best, love the people we are blessed to have in our lives and aim for the highest standards of truth. We are only human, but perhaps through love we rise above our humanness and experience a gift of purity that captures our hearts and gives flight to our souls.

Thank you, Papa and Mama, for thinking of me as a miracle and treating me as such. I may have started off a bit scared, but I have learned love overcomes all and I go to bed each night and I do dream sweet dreams.

Made in the USA
San Bernardino, CA
19 April 2014